They tell me to be the

with shadows easily seen.

I tell them I am each hour,

every phase of the sun and moon.

Writing Poetry with Middle School Students

Kindle the Fire

They tell me to be a lake

They will stock me with ideas,

so their catch is guaranteed.

I tell them I am the ocean

SHELLEY TUCKER, PH.D.

tumble-tossed in sandy hands,

spilling in all directions.

GOOD YEAR BOOKS

Pearson Learning Group

ACKNOWLEDGMENTS

Thank you so much to the following teachers for their excellent support of this work: Mary Edwards, Joel Gillman, Jill Meyers, Greg Jones, Tamara Bunnell, Dana Absgarten, Peter Sarurda, Francis Finan, Lori Eickelberg, Michael Danielson, Sara Yamaski, Kay Greenberg, and the teachers, staff, and parents at McGilvra, a Seattle Public School.

I am indebted to the work of Naomi Shihab Nye, William Stafford, Mary Oliver, and Billy Collins, who write poems that are at once profound and accessible; to Kenneth Koch, Donald Graves, Natalie Goldberg, Anne Lamott, Tim Hulley, George Lakoff, and Mark Johnson for their teachings about writing and thinking.

My special thanks to the Seattle Arts Commission for its award of an Arts in Education grant, supporting the development of this work.

Thank you Kelly Koechel, age 16, for creating the name of this book, *Kindle the Fire*.

My deepest appreciation to my friends and family in poetry: Lauren Wilson, Claudia Mauro, Caitlin Wilson, John Poole, Rosalie Gammelgaard, and Nancy Talley; to Patrick Crowley, for our celebrations of words and voice; to my granddaughter, Jackie, a living poem; and to my wonderful husband, Bruce Sherman, who loves like the finest poem of all.

This book is dedicated to my mother, Chickie Kitchman, for her unwavering belief in the artistry of children.

The following people have contributed to the development of this product:
Art & Design: M. Jane Heelan, Liz Nemeth
Editorial: Cindy Kane
Manufacturing: Mark Cirillo, Thomas Dunne
Production: Karen Edmonds, Jennifer Murphy
Publishing Operations: Carolyn Coyle

ISBN 0-673-61732-7
Printed in the United States of America
1 2 3 4 5 6 7 8 9   06 05 04 03 02 01

This Book Is Printed
on Recycled Paper

1-800-321-3106
www.pearsonlearning.com

Table of contents

They tell me to be the day
with shadows easily seen.

I tell them I am each hour,
every phase of the sun and moon.

They tell me to be a lake.

They will stock me with ideas,

so their catch is guaranteed.

I tell them I am the ocean,

tumble-tossed in sandy hands,

spilling in all directions.

Introduction

POETRY WRITING IS AN INVITATION. It encourages students to think and write creatively, use poetic language in speech and prose, see new connections between the things around them, appreciate beauty, pay attention, and listen attentively. Poetry writing gives students a way to describe nature, express humor, examine relationships, review the past, frame a moment, write about the future, and ask and answer questions. It is an ideal part of the language arts curriculum because it is both a creative art form and an academic discipline.

This book offers a map for writing **free verse poetry** (poems without end rhyme or set structures) that is relevant, interesting, and exciting. Every student, regardless of academic accomplishment, can excel in writing free verse poetry because it is based on everyday thoughts, experiences, feelings, and language. Topics are offered on the reproducible handouts in this book, but students may use nearly any subject in their poems. In general, the easier handouts in a section appear at the beginnings of chapters. Lines are provided on the handouts for students' poems, but in many cases, writers will need extra paper to fully develop their ideas.

The poetry writing exercises in *Kindle the Fire* encourage students to discover similarities between unlike things, use parts of speech in new ways, and develop their ideas through sound and imagery. The exercises will teach and challenge middle school students, and they are also a valuable resource for older elementary school children, high school students, and beginning adult writers. All of the student poetry was written in my classes. Many of the poems are by middle school students; however, the poets range in age from eight through adult. These poems show that free verse poetry gives writers a wide variety of choices. This includes the optional use of titles.

Editing for content

Writers carefully **edit** the words in their poems to make meanings precise and sounds effective. When editing, they can pay particular attention to specific words and lines that feel wrong to them. Instead of reworking an entire poem, they might start with these areas. Their goal then is to maintain the original flow of their writing while finding accurate words to convey exactly what they mean.

The intentional repetition of words in a poem shows that sound is an integral part of meaning. Poets consider the repetition of all words, even small ones, such as *the* and *a.* Ask your students to read their poems aloud to themselves and others to hear whether repeated words support the sounds, rhythms, and meanings of their poems.

Inflectional endings, such as *ing, er,* and *ed,* added to root verbs (e.g., *call* and *open*) influence the sound and movement of poetry. As students edit their poems, they might consider verb forms with and without inflectional endings. Just varying the verb *walk,* for example, changes the sound and impact of these sentences: *I am walking in the snow. I walk in the snow.*

Students might also consider the number of syllables in the last word of each **stanza** (group of lines separated by a space). Single syllable words (e.g., *rock* and *talk*) and compound words in which each syllable is strongly stressed (e.g., *schoolhouse* and *backyard*) provide strong endings. Multisyllabic words (e.g., *investigate* and *laughter*) that do not end with a stressed syllable offer softer endings. Some poets end at least half of their stanzas with single syllable or compound words for emphasis and closure.

The first definition of a poem found in a dictionary usually states that it is a piece of writing expressing a strong feeling or sentiment. Poets might use this property as an ally when editing their writing by asking: Does the poem feel right? Am I conveying exactly what I want to say? Are my descriptions precise? Are my ideas original and not overused in other people's writing?

Editing for format and conventions

The line breaks, capitalization, punctuation, and **format** in free verse poetry are determined by the writer. Until recently, nearly all poets **capitalized** the first letters of lines and proper nouns. Most poets today, however, capitalize only the first letter in a sentence (rather than a line) and the beginning letter in proper nouns, as in prose writing. I have students **punctuate poems** in this way when I teach poetry in schools. This makes their poems more readable while simultaneously reinforcing the writing conventions of prose.

Line breaks (where the lines in a poem end) provide pauses, stops, and emphases, serving as effective and important means of punctuation and stress in free verse poetry. An easy way for students to end a line is to stop it where they pause to breathe. Many poets always put the article (e.g., *a, the*) on the same line as the noun it is modifying (e.g., *the moon, a basketball*). Writers generally place the preposition and its object (e.g., *by the bridge* and *on the table*) on the same line. Try this exercise with your students. First, select a poem. Then ask your students to rewrite it a few times, changing where the lines end without altering the words. They'll see that the placement of words on a line can dramatically change the meaning of poetry.

The format or layout of a poem serves as its container. Similar to a picture frame around a photograph, the format can completely alter the sense of the poem. Most writers today present their poetry flush left. Other presentations need to support the meaning of the poem.

Publishing

Students can publish poetry books with staples, comb bindings, stitches, spiral bindings, or glue. No matter what form students' books take, it is important for them to publish their writing. During the publishing process, students hone the craft of poetry, considering, revising, and correcting the words, spelling, format, and punctuation. Books are validation of their work, allowing them to appreciate their poetry while sharing their creativity with others.

Readings

Ask your students to read their poems aloud. Student poetry speaks to wide audiences because of the relevance of its topics, use of figurative language and sound, relatively short length, sentiments expressed, and opportunity for authentic expression. Poetry writing, listening, and sharing build community and caring in the classroom.

Metaphor

The comparison of two unlike nouns

A METAPHOR is the comparison of two nouns with different meanings. *Music is chocolate, love was a paper clip,* and *the vocabulary of a river* are examples of metaphors. The nouns in metaphors evoke our senses, providing immediate and tangible experience. Read the word *chocolate,* for example, and you can almost see, taste, feel, smell, and touch it. In the metaphor *music is chocolate,* music takes on the tantalizing attributes of chocolate—rich, thick, filling, and leaving you wanting more.

The power of metaphors does not derive from the use of large or obscure nouns. Instead, students start with everyday nouns, such as *tree, pencil, night,* and *peach.* Then they make unique comparisons, as in *a tree is an octopus* or *a pencil is a river.* The impact of metaphors comes from the two nouns poets choose to compare and how they expand these ideas in their writing.

Nouns in metaphors do something adjectives can't. They serve as compasses, showing poets how to direct their writing. In the sentences *music is interesting, our vacation was fun,* and *my anger was bad,* the adjectives *interesting, fun,* and *bad* do not summon our senses or provide concrete information. Change the adjectives to nouns, however, and many paths for poems emerge. In the metaphors *our vacation was a roller coaster* and *my anger was a pomegranate,* the characteristics of the nouns *roller coaster* and *pomegranate* provide writers with specific ideas for poetry. A student could easily extend these metaphors and write, for example, *our vacation was a roller coaster, slow to start but quickly offering a panorama of sights* and *my anger was a lemon with a thick skin and sour taste.*

Metaphors ignite writing with original ideas. Initially, though, some poets lose the power of metaphors in two ways. First, instead of comparing two nouns that are different, they connect similar nouns, as in *music is sound* and *tears are feelings*, composing definitions rather than metaphors. Second, some poets write metaphors they've already heard, such as *time is money* and *heart of gold*. Because overused comparisons offer nothing new, writers rarely develop these metaphors in their poems.

Students can easily avoid these problems by writing original comparisons and using two nouns with different meanings in their metaphors. To illustrate these points, you might try this exercise with your class. Write the words *music is* on the left side of the board or transparency. In the middle of the board, write the following categories: *animals, fruit, vegetables, seasons, holidays, weather, sports, transportation, feelings, things in the sky*, and *objects in the ocean*. On the right side of the board write, *Where? When? Why? How? Doing what?* Tell your students that they are going to compare music to nouns with different meanings. At first this might seem a little unusual, but they will quickly see that the comparison of any two nouns can always be explained. Review with them how the composition of new metaphors differs from definitions and overused comparisons.

Then start at the top of the category list and ask your students to compare music to animals, as in *music is a snake* and *music is a cat*. Next, have them make their sentences longer by answering one of the questions on the right side of the board to create, for example, *music is a snake, coiling around my mind* and *music is a cat with changing moods.* (You might suggest that they lengthen their sentences without the word *because,* which sounds better in prose than poetry.) Then ask them to make comparisons between music and types of fruit, as in *music is a watermelon with the juice of inspiration* and *music is blueberries that I eat in handfuls*. Have your students continue to explore connections between music and words from many different categories.

Students will have fun writing metaphors and will discover that the possibilities for original comparisons are exciting and endless. Metaphors offer poets a terrain of new ideas while helping them map the direction of their poetry.

Imagine Time Is a Tomato

On the lines below, write **unusual** comparisons by adding the names of animals, bodies of water, feelings, seasons, transportation, months, musical instruments, or other places and things. Then complete your sentences.

EXAMPLES: Imagine this pen is a river, ink of ideas flowing over rocky words.
Imagine time is a ripe apple, rolling quickly down a hill.

You may change any of the nouns printed on the lines.

Imagine a storm is _____

_____

Imagine the wind is _____

_____

Imagine thunder is _____

_____

Imagine lightning is _____

_____

Imagine rain is _____

_____

Imagine stars are _____

_____

Imagine the sun is _____

_____

Imagine the sky is _____

_____

 On another sheet of paper, write one of your *imagine* sentences, and compose a poem about it. You may also use a number of related *imagine* sentences in the same poem.

IMAGINE WEATHER

Imagine a storm is glass,
shattering on a metal plate.
Imagine the wind is the billowing dress
of the sun, cooling off.
Imagine thunder is a giant baby,
wanting the milk of the clouds.
Imagine lightning is the turtle of the sky
with a bad hair day.

◆ RYAN RANTUREAU, age 10

FOOD OF IMAGINATION

Imagine lightning is fire
on your burnt bread.
Imagine wind is syrup
blowing onto your toast.
Imagine rain is apples
falling from the sky.
Imagine stars are kiwis
from the old fruit tree.
Imagine the sky
is jumping into your mouth.

◆ RICHARD SUAREZ, age 14

Imagine this day is a sweater,
its warm yarny fingers stretching
your mind across its cloth.

Imagine this stone is a candle,
a strong wick of an unknown land,
the scales of a fish or even a woolen sock,
something that is one thing
and still another.

Imagine this poem is a leopard,
the strange cat stretches out
over the spinning landscape
as it bounces across the land.

◆ SARAH GREINER, age 9

Imagine sand is the dry scalp of your head.
Imagine waves are s'mores at a campfire.
Imagine the sea is a glass of water
coming out of your faucet.
Imagine the sun is a vacation for two
at the Bahamas.
Imagine Earth is spaghetti
raveled up on your fork.
Imagine this poem is the break of day
and the dawn of a new time.

◆ TRAVIS WELLS, age 11

IMAGINE

Imagine this salmon is a fire,
colors as vibrant as the sun
flapping smoothly in the air.
The salmon soars, fire against wind,
maintaining its speed.

There is a fire within that salmon,
and it can come to you, too,
if you only imagine.

◆ JODY BLASKI, age 12

They Tell Me to Be a Window

On the lines below, **write nouns (places, things, and ideas)**. You might name bodies of water, transportation, holidays, things in the ocean, objects in the sky, feelings, seasons, months, and times of the day. Then complete your sentences.

E X A M P L E :   They tell me to be the day
with shadows easily seen.
I tell them I am each hour,
every phase of the sun and moon.
They tell me to be a lake.
They will stock me with ideas,
so their catch is guaranteed.
I tell them I am the ocean,
tumble-tossed in sandy hands,
spilling in all directions.

They tell me to be _____

_____

I tell them I am _____

_____

They tell me to be _____

_____

I tell them I am _____

_____

They tell me to be _____

_____

I tell them I am _____

_____

They tell me to be _____

_____

I tell them I am _____

_____

They tell me to be water running crystal clear.
They don't know I can hardly swim.

I tell them I am a big city,
needing people to make the day.
I am the lost wanderer
trying to find my place.

They tell me to be a machine,
programming my ways,
a tight screw to ease my vulnerable pains.

I tell them I am a vulture
waiting for a cadaver to crawl my way,
circling the dying sounds
on a string of fears.

◆ SHIELLA CALDEJON, age 13

THEY TELL ME

They tell me to be the moon, shining over everyone
who doesn't see what's in front of him.
I tell them I am the sun,
giving light and showing the way.

They tell me to be a house
with warmth, shelter, and safety.
I tell them I am a fence,
keeping you in and leaving danger out.

They tell me to be an old man,
wise, all-knowing, cherished, admired.
I tell them I am a young boy, curious,
wanting to know the world around me,
looking for an answer.

They tell me to be a book,
all the answers inside, waiting to be discovered.
I tell them I am an author,
just wait and see what happens.

They tell me to be the best kept secret, unique,
mysterious, something everyone wants to know about.
I tell them I am a word, foreign and understood,
all at the same time.

◆ VINCENT HO, age 12

They tell me to be the night
with stars of brightness and hope.
I tell them I am the clouds
with darkness covering the sky.
They tell me to be a tree
with branches of strength.
I tell them I am a squirrel
who hides its power in the tree's womb.
They tell me to be a horse
strong and trampling the earth.
I tell them I am the reins
trying to drive myself into power.

◆ PARAK ESHETU, age 15

TELLING

They tell me to be a flower, standing and growing tall, full of promise.
I tell them I am a butterfly, moving with magnificent color and freedom.
I tell them I am flying from flower to flower inhaling its beauty.
They tell me to be a car, reliable, sturdy, and dependable.
They fill me with gas and oil, promising a smooth ride with no breakdowns.
I tell them I am a child who will give the best dependability my fuel will allow.

◆ KATIE BUSHNELL, age 15

Music Is a Bus (first page)

Complete some of the following comparisons by **writing nouns**. You might name animals, things in the sky, sports, colors, holidays, transportation, months, weather, bodies of water, things in your refrigerator, fruits, vegetables, seasons, and objects in the ocean.

E X A M P L E :   Time is a chocolate.
                       A nightmare is an alligator.

Make your sentences longer by answering: Where? When? Why? or Doing what?

E X A M P L E :   Time is a chocolate, tasting good and gone too soon.
                       A nightmare is an alligator as it chomps away at my restful sleep.

You may change the nouns at the front of the lines and use other ones instead.

Music is _____

Money is _____

Television is _____

Love is _____

I am _____

Time is _____

Soccer is _____

Basketball is _____

A car is _____

A nightmare is _____

The moon is _____

A dream is _____

Summer vacation is _____

School is _____

Music Is a Bus (second page)

Write one of your comparisons from the first page on the line:

_____

List words that describe the **second noun** in your comparison:

_____   _____

_____   _____

E X A M P L E :   Life is a basketball
C O M P A R I S O N (M E T A P H O R)

bounce

hoops

passes

Michael Jordan

practice

Use some or all of the words from your list in a poem about the **first noun** in your comparison. Use other words, too. Include your comparison in your poem, probably as the first line.

_____

_____

_____

_____

_____

_____

_____

_____

THE MOON

The moon is a cookie, half eaten and another half to go.
The moon can be soft, crisp, and hard all at the same time.
It is milk poured into a big bowl of flour
with pecans falling like stars from the sky.
The moon feels like walnuts dug out of shells
and tastes like chocolate in a silver wrapper.
The moon is baked in a steaming, hot oven.
When done, a hand grabs the moon and eats it,
without even letting it cool.

◆ KIANA RHEM, age 10

SOCCER

Soccer is a perfect storm,
waving always moving
never stopping
sunlit waves of motion
breaking on the shore,
flying on its unsinkable raft
of silver light.

◆ GREGORY SMART, age 10

STARS

Stars are grapes waiting to be picked
by little children's hands.
Stars fall as grapes,
fall into children's mouths.
Beautiful, marvelous grapes
hang,
swing,
delicious,
mouthwatering good.

Hanging in the sky,
stars are eaten one by one
as the sun begins to rise.

◆ MARISA MORALES, age 11

THE OCEAN

The ocean is a horse,
powerful and mysterious,
white nostrils quivering,
tail poised in flight.
The crest of the wave is her neck,
her mane the crashing spray.
The ocean's ears flick, flick.
Her haunches twitch,
hocks ready to leap to freedom.
She covers seabirds with her breath
ready for time, the wild-horse trainer.

◆ ABIGAIL FAY, age 14

While I Wasn't Watching, I Became a Pencil

Finish some of the following sentences by adding a **noun**, such as the name of an animal, sport, manufactured item, time of day, season, month, body of water, food, object in the sky, emotion, or thing that grows outside.

E X A M P L E :   While I wasn't watching, the moon became a c.d.

Then make your sentence longer.

E X A M P L E :   While I wasn't watching, the moon became a c.d., spinning the sky's song.

You may change any of the highlighted words printed on the lines.

While I wasn't watching, **time** became _____

_____

While I wasn't watching, **music** became _____

_____

While I wasn't watching, **I** became _____

_____

While I wasn't watching, **you** became _____

_____

While I wasn't watching, **fear** became _____

_____

While I wasn't watching, **night** became _____

_____

While I wasn't watching, **friends** became _____

_____

While I wasn't watching, **this story** became _____

_____

On another sheet of paper, write one of your *while I wasn't watching* sentences, and compose a poem about it. You may also use a number of related *while I wasn't watching* sentences in the same poem.

WHILE I WASN'T WATCHING

While I wasn't watching, music became a speck of sand
roaming through the underbrush of the wind.

While I wasn't watching, I became a mountain,
creating dreams, living up to expectations.

While I wasn't watching, the sun became a page,
filling the world with the simple pleasure of faith.

While I wasn't watching, fear became a crystal ball,
telling the fortune of tears, bellowing in the darkness.

While I wasn't watching, this story became a puddle,
dirty as a street, yet fine as a thread in the blanket of my life.

◆ VINCEA VALENTINA WILLARD, age 14

GRANITE

While I wasn't watching, I became a rock,
picked up, hurled, and chipped,
smoothed by time, then skipped.
Hard as sand,
my beauty lies in my granite.

◆ SCOTT CHILBERG, age 13

DICTIONARY

While I wasn't watching,
my heart became a dictionary,
pages flipping full of new descriptive words.
While I wasn't watching,
my heart became the alphabet
spelling out the way.

◆ ELIZABETH McKEE, age 12

While I wasn't watching, time became grass swaying with the wind
going by slowly, like a ten-year-old's summer vacation
when three months seems like an eternity,
playing on a jungle gym until the sound
of your mother calls from a far distance.
While I wasn't watching, time moved like a video game,
never stopping except for one sound
of a faint voice lying in her bed.
While I wasn't watching, time became still
like a frozen statue made of the rock
from which the earth was conceived.

◆ CAMERON VELORIA, age 12

Call This Pen a River (first page)

Choose a **subject** for your poem, such as a sport, musical instrument, feeling, place, body of water, something that grows outside, object in the sky, or a season.

Then make lists of **things** related to your subject, as in the following example:

E X A M P L E :   basketball
[S U B J E C T]

    basketball
    pass
    score
    time-out
    backboard
    rim

S U B J E C T : _____

List **things** related to your subject on the following lines:

_____

_____

_____

_____

_____

On the lines on the next page, add the names of the **things** from your lists.

Compare these to other completely **different** things, places, and feelings (as shown in bold print in the example below), and then make your sentences longer.

E X A M P L E :

    Call a basketball the sun, rimming around a universe of sports.
    Call a pass a river, arcing over applause.
    Call the score an ocean, changing the currents of the game.
    Call a time-out ingredients, a new recipe for play.
    Call the backboard a hand, guiding the ball into the hoop.
    Call the rim the moon, reflecting our hopes.

Call This Pen a River (second page)

Write a word from your list from the previous page on each of the following lines.
Then compare what you've named to things that are completely different,
and make your sentences longer.

Call _____

_____

Call _____

_____

Call _____

_____

Call _____

_____

Call _____

_____

Call _____

_____

Use your favorite lines in a poem, or choose one or two lines and expand those ideas:

_____

_____

_____

_____

_____

_____

 _____

A CRUSH

Call a crush a cross-country race.
Call eye contact the warm-up.
Call talking the middle of the race
when you aren't sure if she likes you.
Call flirtation the last stretch.
You are running full speed
and think you are going to win.

Call the news that she doesn't like you
the part where you trip on a root, stumble ten feet,
and smack your head into a pine tree,
dazed and partially conscious.
She regards you with curiosity,
marveling at the enormous lump on your forehead.
◆ VAN VU, age 15

BASKETBALL

Call the ball an orange going through a gaping hole.
Call the rim a mouth, waiting to be filled.
Call the crowd a huge piece of chocolate,
making the players hyper.
Call a time-out the key to open the rim and win the game.
Call the floor the world, waiting to be used.
Call a pass the friendship between two players,
working together to score.
◆ VICTOR LINDSTROM, age 11

SKIING

Call a ski a slithering snake,
sliding down the slope.
Call the snow a hard cloud
under your feet.
Call a chairlift an escalator
in the cold breeze.
Call goggles a reflection of yourself
going down a hill.
Call a pole a spear,
digging into the snow.
Call a glove a handful of warmth
as the cold bounces off it.
◆ ERIC HAGEN, age 10

MUSIC

Call music a conversation,
a dialogue between instruments.
Call the notes footprints,
leading the music.
Call a concert a rainstorm,
a torrential downpour of sound.
Call the crowd a slate,
music etched upon their minds.
◆ DEREK BOTHEREAN, age 16

VOLLEYBALL

Call a volleyball a swell on the ocean.
Call a pass a tossing wave.
Call a spike the breaker,
slamming into the ocean surface.
Call the players ships, scrambling to beat the waves.
Call the game the restless weather,
capable of changing direction at any moment.
◆ JENNIFER SALEMANN, age 15

I Wear the Computer

On the lines below, start your poem with the words:

I wear (the)

Then complete your sentence, **adding the name of a thing other than clothes.**
For example:

book	hope	January	elephant
computer	fear	volcano	tiger
television	peace	winter	friendship
telephone	love	night	baseball
homework	time	ocean	piano

Write a poem about your idea.

EXAMPLE: TIME
I wear time like a necklace,
grab each link
and try to climb it as a rope.
But there is no peak,
and I become a mouse,
racing around and around
on my circular track of scarcity.

_____

_____

_____

_____

_____

_____

_____

_____

_____

LOVE OF THE GAME

I wear the baseball diamond

like a suit of armor,

the dirt as a cloak and grass as cleats.

I strap them on

to do battle against other teams.

When I wear them, I am invincible.

Nothing can touch me unless I say it can.

Nothing can affect me without my permission.

The baseball gods flow through me

from my head to toes.

◆ KEVIN GARBER, age 13

WEARING THE OCEAN

I wear the ocean as a suit,

and put on waves like blue pants

that flow like a river.

I wear a fish as a hat,

wagging like a tail.

I put on sand like a shirt,

golden and rough.

I wear seaweed as my jacket,

flowing in the wind.

◆ MARIA PRONICHEVA, age 10

MY LIFE?

I wear my life as if I don't own it.

A borrowed coat on a chilly night,

it doesn't quite fit.

My life's a little too soft and fluffy,

not at all what I would choose.

◆ ALEENA WALKER, age 14

PRISONER

I wear the homework

like chains of a prisoner.

The heavy weight drags me down,

distracting me from the phone.

Work, work, work,

think, think, think,

write, write, write,

are all that I do.

My mother locks me in this prison cell,

torturing me with the words,

No calls until the homework is done.

I want to rip off this homework,

bury it, destroy it.

But these are my permanent clothes.

◆ OLIVIA HERRING, age 14

PEACE

I wear peace like earrings.

It sparkles and shines.

I wear it with hope,

healing the burning of hate.

My earrings of peace

help me destroy

any necklace or string of lies.

◆ CARMEN M. VIGIL, age 11

NAME _____

Alligator of Hope Smiles Its Toothy Grin

Choose an animal from the following lists or select a different animal:

Dog of	Gorilla of	Rat of	Giraffe of
Cat of	Eagle of	Mouse of	Lion of
Salmon of	Snake of	Hippo of	Kangaroo of

Then add the name of a feeling. The following are some possibilities:

hope	promise	laughter	peace
rage	guilt	fear	ambition
forgiveness	joy	courage	worry

Write a poem about the feeling, using the characteristics of the animal to describe it.

EXAMPLE: FEAR
The rat of fear scurries
through back pockets of worry.
I set traps placed at the doorsills of memory,
living cages, designed for easy catch and release.
But this fear is elusive and grows
as shadows merge with form.
Soon room-sized cages become necessary,
and I am the gate it must enter,
rat after rat scratching its way to the surface.

SNAKE OF DECEPTION

I know the snake of deception.
It slithers every time they open their mouths.
Not slimy, but scaly, its jagged tongue cuts the air.
They say it is not a real snake
but a fake one made of rubber.
Yet I know that it is ready to coil around me and squeeze
until I cannot see right from wrong
or truth from lies.
◆ PREETMA KOONER, age 16

GREED

The snake of greed coils
its body around man,
hissing, whispering
promises of success and profit.

All the while, greed's coil
grows tighter and tighter
squeezing the last drops of our humanity
into its green wake.
◆ DREW CASON, age 16

DRAGON OF CURIOSITY

The dragon of curiosity pries everywhere,
its sharp mouth grinning
when it finds a new discovery.

Occasionally, it smiles
when it sees something
not meant for its scaly mind.
But more often it laughs
with the joy of new knowledge.

My dragon is always growing,
hungry to learn.

Is yours?
◆ BENJAMIN GRAVES, age 11

EAGLE OF COURAGE

The eagle of courage
soars through the trees
of the forest moon.
I take a gun which has numbers of memory,
a painful weapon, designed to kill.
But the courage of the eagle still lives
like the legends of other animals.
The gun is fully cocked and ready,
and I am the bush it will soar by,
screaming as it scrapes the surface.
◆ RYAN LOVELAND, age 13

RAGE

The lion of rage tramples
through the forest of pain.
His powerful growl sets fire
to the ears of his prey.
He kills the mouse of worry
and enjoys its bittersweet taste of fear.
He is the king of the wilderness of emotions,
consuming all in his path,
kindling his webs of sadness and hate.
◆ MARY VINUELAS, age 15

He Carries Laughter in a Suitcase

Start your poem with the words:

I/We/They/He/She

carry/carries

Then add an emotion or human condition. The following are some possibilities:

this moment	the future	laughter	prejudice
peace	worry	friendship	promise
war	hope	the past	arguments

Choose one of the following or name another container to complete the sentence:

briefcase	envelope	paper bag	lunch bag
suitcase	backpack	knapsack	purse

On the following lines, write a poem about the feeling or human condition, **using the traits of the container.**

EXAMPLE OF
A FIRST LINE: We carry prejudice in our backpacks like leaking pepper spray.

_____

_____

_____

_____

_____

_____

_____

_____

_____

_____

_____

PROMISE

He carries forgiveness in his pocket
like a myth or a fairy tale with a happy ending.
His wife carries laughter like the sun going down
and the moon coming up in the dark blue sky.
Their daughter, with silky hair the color of space,
carries a purse like a teacher with a box of chalk.
Inside she holds promise,
like an ice cream cone on a hot summer day.

◆ STEPHANIE JACKSON, age 10

RACES

They carry the hum in their briefcases.
They carry the drum in their suits.
They carry the repression in their faces.
They carry their nature in the loot.

Off they go to the races
Not knowing they are the root
Of all the dead spaces
Running for the same absolute.

◆ DANIEL GALLOWAY, age 17

WAR

They carry war on their shoulders.
They grasp hate in their hands.
They bring disgust in their hearts.
They rest anger on their backs.

But we let this happen.
We let it occur.
We are part of they
Until war goes away.

◆ KJIERSTIN RAMSING, age 16

GOODWILL

We carry friendship in our paper bag
and let it seep out onto the ground of prejudice,
turning arguments into laughter.

He carries the past in his briefcase
and opens it whenever he wants
to remember the happy times.

She carries forgiveness in her purse
to heal annoyance and greed.

They carry peace in their envelope,
and use it against war.
When they open it,
it erupts into pieces of promise.

◆ CARMEN M. VIGIL, age 11

MOMENT

They carry this moment in a bag,
opening and gobbling its contents
in a mad hunger before lunch.
Some let the moment sit in their lockers rotting
not knowing what is growing inside,
while others just throw the moment away.

◆ DANIEL SMILEY, age 15

Personification

The assignment of human traits to things

When poets write P E R S O N I F I C A T I O N , they make things seem like people. *That flashlight winked, the serious stars,* and *voice of my pencil* are examples of personification. This poetic technique highlights some of the finest features of poetry. It creates vivid and immediate imagery using an economy of words.

Personification is a type of metaphor because it implies anything is a person. With metaphors, writers can use one noun to depict another. The same principle applies to personification, as poets describe things as people.

Students like writing personification because the guidelines for it are straightforward and the content of their poetry emerges immediately. First, students choose subjects other than people and animals for their poems. Then they give their topics human traits. A variety of ways to create personification are listed below.

How to write personification:

1. Use human actions to describe things.

> **E X A M P L E S :**   The basketball *smiles*.
>
>   Time *is singing*.

2. Give things human body parts.

> **E X A M P L E S :**   The *hands* of the sun
>
>   The stapler's *teeth*

3. Use human adjectives to describe things.

> **E X A M P L E S :**   *Honest* car
>
>   A *courageous* computer

4. Assign clothing and jewelry to things.

> E X A M P L E S :   The football wears a *leather coat*.
>
> I hold the *gloves* of sound.

5. Give things friends and family.

> E X A M P L E S :   Pink's *parents are red and white*.
>
> Love's *best friend is kindness*.

6. Create a complete personality for things. Give them jobs, hobbies, dreams, fears, work, favorite foods, and homes.

> E X A M P L E S :   The drum *vacations* by the sea.
>
> Stars *live in sky apartments*.

7. Refer to things using personal pronouns, such as *she, he, her,* and *his* instead of *it*.

> E X A M P L E S :   The ocean waved *her* arms.
>
> The potato winked *his* eyes.

In general, personification poems are strongest when students focus on single topics, such as winter or a computer. This creates cohesive personalities for the objects they personify. When students write, instead, about a constellation of related subjects, such as snow, sleds, and January or a keyboard, monitor, and screen, their poetry can seem disjointed or superficial.

The human traits poets give to things need to make sense for the poems to work. While the personification *a football wears a skirt made of ivy* sounds interesting, it has no congruent meaning. The personification *a football wears a leather coat,* however, does makes sense. As a result, the football takes on a personality suggested by its clothes.

With personification, things are given added dimensions. A tree emerges as a person with branches for arms and roots as legs. The tree finds work in gardens and forests, sometimes posing as a painter's model. As the poet shows a tree's hopes and fears, the reader sees the tree from a new perspective. Do trees really have thoughts, feelings, friends, and dreams? Personification assures us that the answer is yes.

The Stone's Hair Is Made of Moss

Make a thing seem like a person. Choose one of the following words or select a different **topic that's not a person or an animal:**

a mountain	a season	a computer	hope
the ocean	a star	music	war
the moon	fire	soccer	laughter
night	earth	football	anger

Then write a poem on the lines below, giving your topic human actions and human body parts. The following are some possibilities:

hears	remembers	laughs	hair
breathes out	sees	sings	eyes
listens to	dreams about	cries	teeth
smiles	dances	exercises	heart
inhales	talks	writes	fingers

Use the words *she, he, her, him, his,* and *hers* instead of *it* and *its* when you refer to your topic.

EXAMPLE: FIRE
Fire has feet of ashes and arms of flames.
She lives in the smallest match and the greatest idea.
Fire holds creativity in her hands
as she helps it catch light.
There is fire in the coldest icicle,
prisms of hot possibility melting into streams of inspiration.
So the next time you see a stone, a tree, or a rose,
look for the fire within, ready to ignite your mind.

THEY CALL HER NIGHT

She creeps across the evening skies,
Exercising her arms and stretching her thighs.
Her fingers reach every corner of the world.
Her dark flowing hair is twisted and twirled.
She takes a deep breath and swallows the light,
Then breathes out the dark. They call her the night.

◆ SARAH COOLEY, age 14

SPRING

Spring smiles to me and laughs
through her hair of wind.
Spring talks to me as she kneels down to kiss me.
Her hands create flowers from the ground,
not like her cousin, winter,
who destroys everything in sight.

Spring leaps and bounds through the woods.
Her laugh is a crystal clear stream of happiness
as she slowly gives way to her brother, summer.

◆ AARON LOUX, age 12

WINTER

Winter remembers every smile of any child
who has made a snowman,
hears laughter from the grandkids
as they make snow angels,
laughs when he sees the adults
muttering when school is out,
and tells every little boy or girl who is lonely,
"It will be all right."

◆ CHRIS FORTIER, age 12

POETRY HIDES

Poetry hides in dew-covered roses
and changes with the fairies.
Poetry hides in chocolate
ready to tell your tongue words to say.

You can find poetry in the rain
speaking in a rhythm as she jumps on a tin can.
You see her smiling
as she drifts away with the fog.

Poetry spies from the shafts of light
coming from the window.
Poetry dresses in a gown
of rose scents and shoes of water ripples.

She plays in fields of laughter.
She drinks out of buttercups only in the spring.
You can find poetry in a sparkling raindrop
hiding inside a rose.

◆ SARAH HOLDER, age 11

Blue Inhales Sound

Choose a color. Then tell what it:

hears	inhales	smells	remembers	understands
touches	exhales	feels	speaks	tells
sees	tastes	knows	eats	thinks

Use the words *she, he, her, him, his,* and *hers* instead of *it* and *its* when you write about your color.

E X A M P L E :   GREEN

> Green smells the trees and remembers summer evenings
> > when the touch of bark turned the night black.
>
> Green tells the news of lawns,
> > of worms and dew, and listens with a smile
> > > as dollar bills brag about their worth.
>
> Green is the season of belief
> > when the world becomes imagination
> > > and the canvas of your mind sprouts
> > > > and grows wild.

PURPLE

Purple inhales light like a vacuum eating up dust
and storms around with his head in the sky,
snapping at the stars.
Purple keeps firefly candles
while listening to an orchestra of crickets.

When purple gets angry,
lightning flashes out of the sky.
His eyes, like moons,
watch over earth
in a grizzled band of color.

◆ DANIEL KERVRAN, age 10

TANGERINE

This tangerine presents itself
with an assuring lightness of heart.
Bright and soft
she understands our interests
and our reservations.
Her yellow sees the sun.
Her orange warms the body.
Her red ignites the heart.
But beware!
When she speaks,
it can be bittersweet.

◆ MAX MENATH, age 16

YELLOW

Yellow dances in the sunbeams
on a hot summer day.
He burns my back when I go swimming
and laughs at my helpless scratching.
When nighttime comes, he retreats
to the fluorescent lights of Hollywood,
then wraps himself around the school bus
and watches the black pavement
laying out the road before him.

◆ DANA GOLDEN, age 10

ORANGE

Orange blazes with intensity
hot and scorched
on a blackened playground.
Soundless, fiery fingers
play the bones of the dead.

Burning orange fumes
coalesce in the parched dry throat
of the weary.
Tasteless fire dances along the tongue,
blistering with every step.

◆ KELLY KOECHEL, age 16

RED SPILLS

Red spills out gossip
through the ears of yellow.
Then he slips out secrets
which turn her a bit orange.

◆ TANI IKEDA, age 13

Chocolate Wakes at Dawn with Nightmares of Too Many Nuts

Choose a **food**. Then **make it seem like a person** by giving it some sleep-related human actions. The following are some possibilities:

rises	dreams	has nightmares	snores
goes to sleep	wakes	sleeps	is afraid of the dark

Use the words *she, he, her, him, his,* and *hers* instead of *it* and *its* when you write about your food.

E X A M P L E :   PICKLES

Sometimes, pickles are afraid to sleep.
They remember nightmares
of beds on hamburger buns
and being smothered in mounds
of ketchup as red as hunger.

The sound in your kitchen
is not the purr of the refrigerator.
Open the door and you'll hear the pickles snore
in their homes of brine,
dreaming of earlier times
as cucumbers.

NOODLES

Noodles have dreams full of sauces
and hope melted cheese or beautiful red toppings
will ooze all over them.
But nightmares soon follow these wishes,
fears of humans gobbling them up.
Sometimes they sleep in and realize with horror...
someone is calling,
Dinner is ready. We're having noodles.

SALAD WITH DRESSING

Salad wakes, annoyed that his friend dressing
is poking him in the side again.
Dressing remembers how he used to be ingredients
but now is only a topping.
Dressing shivers from the cold of the fridge.
He tries to sleep, and finally they both drift off,
hoping they will be delicious together.

◆ SYLVIE KREKOW, age 10

SPAGHETTI HOPES

Spaghetti wakes from nightmares of meatballs
and people smothering him in sauce.

He remembers days
when parmesan cheese covered him
and children slurped him through their teeth
like double chocolate milkshakes.

He hopes for nights of sleep
and dreams of garlic bread at his side.

◆ CARMEN M. VIGIL, age 11

BANANAS

Bananas have nightmares.
The degradation of being pureed with the likes
of strawberries, blueberries, and inferior fruit,
carelessly chucked into a blender with its vicious blades
and spun, chopped, and liquefied until there is no banana
but only a faint dream of what once was.
Oh! To be put into ice cream
and feel the cool creaminess drip over it
and the contrast of the hot, hot, fudge....

The only downside is that it's called a banana split.
So cruel a disemboweling is sadly required.
But why? asks the banana. Why split?
Why not have a banana whole?

That is the eternal question.

◆ JESSICA BROWN, age 16

Jaws of the Galaxy (first page)

Use a part of the human body to describe a thing.

Choose a **subject other than a person or an animal,** such as something that grows outside, an object in the sky, a feeling, a sport, a color, a season, music, or a manufactured thing.

Then make lists of **things** related to your subject, as in the following example:

EXAMPLE: trees
[SUBJECT]

        leaves
        branches
        roots
        fruit

SUBJECT: _____
Write the names of **things** that relate to your subject on the following lines:

_____

_____

_____

Add words from your lists on the lines at the bottom of the page. **Then add verbs that do not end with the letters** *ing.* These verbs will help you form complete sentences.

EXAMPLES:

    The arms of autumn **reach** out in many colors to hold October.
    The voice of the tree **takes** root in the gravelly pitch of the earth.

The voice of _____

The eyes of _____

The arms of _____

The teeth of _____

The ribs of _____

The breath of _____

The heart of _____

Jaws of the Galaxy (second page)

On the lines below, write a poem using your favorite sentences from the first page, in an order that makes sense, or develop one of the sentences into a poem.

EXAMPLES: TREE TALK
The voice of the tree takes root
in the gravelly pitch of the earth,
his vocal chords resonant
like the breath of the wind
as he speaks of fallen friends.
The tree talks of forests,
lush with moss and vines,
cut down to make way for roads.

THE HEART OF SOFTBALL

The heart of softball is team togetherness,
the graceful rhythm of a double play,
the beating on the fence
as teammates cheer for each other.
Feeling the pulse of the mechanics
we've so diligently worked on in practice,
to steal—rock and go
to hit—trigger and swing
to play—catch and throw.
And then the passionate moment
the crucial hit with the bases loaded
the diving catch—last out of the game
the slide in home—the winning run.
This is the heart of softball.
This is the love of the game.

◆ CHANCEY ANDERSON, age 15

MYSTERIES

Voices of the pages say, *Read me. Read me*.
The eyes of the books are full of suspense.
Their arms are the titles pulling me to them,
and their teeth chatter
with fear for the characters.

The breath of the genre whispers,
What a mystery,
as the heart of the story beats
for those who love suspense.
The legs of the book run towards me
when I am bored,
the ribs the covers,
holding it all together.

◆ RACHEL RADABAUGH, age 12

DAYBREAK

The rounded shoulders of morning
smooth the new light
Defined curves of strength
awaken gently
Bare sunrise tender to the senses
revives my tired shoulders

◆ SUE TAN, age 16

THE JAWS OF COURAGE

The jaws of courage
clench the mind and eat away all fear.
The strength grasps the heart
and allows confidence to break through.

Courage is strength like calcium,
the sharpness of teeth,
and the will to clamp onto bravery.

◆ KATIE BUSHNELL, age 15

In the Breath of War

Start your poem with one of the following phrases, or use a different body part at the beginning of your writing:

In the hands of   In the eyes of   In the voice of   In the breath of
In the mind of   In the lungs of   In the heart of   In the fingers of

Then add a subject. It might be about a feeling, weather, a season, sport, color, or nature.

EXAMPLE: GLARE
            In the hands of yellow,
            everything seems to shine brightly,
            But in her heart, yellow is blue,
            compromised by green,
            wanting a shadow or earth,
            dark and rich like mud or rust.
            Yellow is tired of singing soprano
            in the chorus of colors.
            So she gathers lemons around her
            and listens as they tell their stories
            before you sweeten them with honey or sugar.

IN THE BODY OF THE EARTH

In the lungs of the earth,
you feel her breathing life to all.
But in her eyes, she sees people
taking her breath for granted.

In the voice of the earth, she cries out
for her people to save and protect her.
But she cries in vain because most ignore her.

Her hands are tired from supporting life,
yet day in and day out she continues to survive
and help her people thrive.

In the mind of the earth she wonders,
Will the day come when I will be respected?
In her heart, she hopes the answer is *yes.*

◆ MEGAN FLAHERTY, age 13

EYES OF AN OAK

In the eyes of an oak, you'll see
memories of hot summer days
of tree houses and swings
of growing children
and camp-outs under the stars.
You'll also see pain,
hard times and suffering,
tears cried beneath these strong limbs,
the birth of new life,
and the blooming of spring.
New generations are born and raised
all in the eyes of an oak.

◆ DANIEL MORGAN, age 13

THE MUSICAL SEEN

In the eyes of music,
the rhythm is seen clearly,
the beats of the music
no matter what style,
punk, rock rap, heavy metal.
He enjoys what he sees,
embracing the notes,
generation after generation.

◆ KEVIN GARBER, age 13

LONGING FOR IDEAS

In the throat of tomorrow, hunger lies in wait
refusing to swallow the hot air that is fed to us.
Blistering ideas are crammed down but not accepted,
swallowing new and unaccustomed morsels of ingenuity,
waiting as the acid in my stomach digests them
into absorbable chunks.
My stomach growls with its need for novelty,
as my throat closes around another paradigm.

◆ SUSANNE WOOLSEY, age 16

The Sky Wears Bracelets Made of Clouds

Choose a **subject** for your poem. The following are some possibilities:

moon	mountain	forest	joy	music
stars	day	sun	fear	homework
sky	rainbow	tree	courage	car
wind	Mars	park	love	airplane

Write a poem, giving your subject some **clothes and jewelry**:

hat	coat	sunglasses	pants	bracelet
shirt	tie	shoes	gloves	diamonds
belt	raincoat	pajamas	watch	rings

Use the words *she, he, her, him, his,* and *hers* instead of *it* and *its* when you refer to your subject.

EXAMPLE: DAY
Day wakes up early
hoping to catch a glimpse of night.
She puts on her hat
and sandals made of dawn.
Day wears a ring on each ray
draping like a yellow scarf of heat across the sky.
Occasionally, she glances at her watch.
Someday, she wants to stay up past dusk.

SHOOTING STAR

Shooting Star is a hot shot

with bell bottoms made of silky strings.

She has long hair of the universe

that gets caught in knots all of the time.

She goes to Starmart and buys moon gel for her hair

and shoes made of rubber platforms.

Then Shooting Star heads to the Universe Theater

with her friends and brags

about how good she was in some movie,

and they all watch her because...

well, she's a star.

◆ REINA KANE, age 10

EARTH'S CLOTHES

Earth's shirt and pants are matching green and blue,

and her belt is as cooked as the equator.

Earth's raincoat protects the fires

from burning out in chimneys.

Her giant sunglasses keep her eyes safe,

and her shoes are as clunky as meteorites.

Earth's hands wave goodnight

as her rings, shaped as stars, sparkle in the dark.

◆ ALEXANDRA FLINT, age 11

THINKING ABOUT DAY

Night goes to sleep so slowly,

thinking about the day.

considering her every move,

wanting to ask her to play.

The sun's golden rings of rays

and her beautiful yellow hair,

What a sight for such a dim light as he,

so the moon thinks about what he wears.

Maybe if I change my apparel,

she'll ask me out someday,

But for now, he says, *I'll just stick*

with thinking about the day.

◆ COURTNEY LOWRY, age 13

PEACE AND RAGE

Peace wears the cloak of hope and courage.

Peace's enemy, Rage, wears a robe

of an avalanche and a howling gale.

They have clashes all the time,

and the universe watches intently.

Rage picks up a river and throws it at Peace.

Peace holds out a tree that lived in the desert.

It gratefully sucks up all the water.

Defeated, Rage sulks off,

once again beaten by good.

◆ RYAN RANTUREAU, age 10

The Bike Has a Vocabulary of Trails

Choose a **subject** other than a person for your poem. The following are some possibilities:

moon	mountain	stone	computer	fear
sky	desert	sun	refrigerator	love
night	rainbow	tree	music	joy
wind	earth	fire	soccer	anger

Then use verbs about thinking, writing, and speaking in a poem to make your subject seem like a person.

spells	uses the grammar of	punctuates	thinks
uses commas	inserts periods	quotes	writes
speaks	has the vocabulary of	recites	capitalizes

EXAMPLE: SEA TALK

The ocean speaks in waves,
getting caught in undercurrents of emotion.
Whales recite Shakespeare
to the soft approval of starfish.
Sand's infinite vocabulary
creates castles of dictionaries.
Jellyfish try to write their biographies,
but their books always seem to lack spine.

DEVELOPMENT

The trees sing no more—
Voices silenced by the dollar sign of the cash register.
Developers tee off bloody stumps oozing sap
And smile for the papers.

The trees no longer speak to each other.
The wind runs over blasted valleys
And empty streams, its denizens slain or fled.
Paved over, the network of their roots no longer reach
To the world's core, to our essential truth.
Is this the developer's dream,
Concrete empire and stagnant sea?

◆ SEAN KINNEMAN, age 16

IN THE DESERT

The fire speaks in flames,
burning its feelings and dreams.
Storms have a vocabulary of raindrops,
washing away memories.
A rainbow thinks in color,
painting your imagination.
The sun breathes light
while exhaling on your face.
The desert capitalizes heat
turning up its scorching attitude.

◆ NINA BORT, age 13

TIDES

The tide has a vocabulary of froth.
White and foaming, she thinks in a rhythmic pulse of salt.
Swaying tendrils of teal weed
recite nursery rhymes to mussels and clams
coaxing them to slowly unhinge
and reveal their pearlescent secrets.
As the jagged rocks enunciate through the grainy waves,
we strain to understand the cryptic message
hidden in the quarrelsome tides.

◆ SUSANNE WOOLSEY, age 16

SPACE TALK

The sun speaks in bright rays,
thrown into the surrounding black universe.
The planets sing softly to the stars.
The emptiness of the galaxy
rewrites the dictionary
in the language of the planets.
Ship debris tries to reunite as one
but the ship is always short of parts.

◆ MICHAEL LEMLEY, age 12

Simile

The comparison of two unlike nouns using the words like or as

A SIMILE is the comparison of two nouns with different meanings, using the words *like* or *as* to make the connection. *Friendship is like ice cream, fear moved like lightning,* and *leaves feel as slippery as fish* are examples of similes.

A simile is a type of metaphor, but similes and true metaphors vary in significant ways. Because the word *like* in a simile implies a variety of possible comparisons, a simile is usually more encompassing but less emphatic than a metaphor. To demonstrate this difference to your students, have them write metaphors. Then ask them to add the word *like,* and compare the similes to their related metaphors, as in the following examples:

Love was like a pomegranate.	simile
Love was a pomegranate.	metaphor
Their anger was like broken glass.	simile
Their anger was broken glass.	metaphor

At first, most students think similes are easier to write than metaphors. Poets, however, often discover that writing strong similes can be quite challenging. This is because the word *like* seems to signal that the comparisons must be literal, as in *pizza is like a gift* or *pizza is like fun*. The goal in composing similes, however, is to write comparisons that seem true and offer new insights, as in *pizzas are like basketballs, soaring through my hoop of hunger* or *pizzas are like time, disappearing quickly.*

Similes look like metaphors. The structure of similes, however, easily expands to include adjectives that function like bridges. In the simile *the grass is as green as money,* for example, the adjective *green* carries the traits of money back to describe grass, making it seem like money, abundant and luxurious.

Describe Constellations Like the Patterns in a Bird's Wings

Describe the words on the lines below **by naming things that are very different**. For example, add the names of animals, transportation, things that grow, seasons, sports, and feelings.

Then make your sentences longer by answering: Where? When? or Doing what?

EXAMPLES: Describe the moon like a goat climbing to the top of a mountain.
Describe a legend like a tree that keeps growing through the years.

You may change any of the nouns printed on the lines.

Describe the sea like _____

_____

Describe the sun like _____

_____

Describe sand like _____

_____

Describe waves like _____

_____

Describe the Earth like _____

_____

Describe the Big Dipper like _____

_____

Describe the Little Dipper like _____

_____

Describe constellations like _____

_____

On another sheet of paper, use some of your **related** lines in a poem. Include other ideas.

DESCRIBE

Describe the Earth like a lollipop turning in a little boy's mouth
and constellations like ideas waiting to be formed.
Describe an eclipse like one moment when anything can come true
and the sun is its heart of happiness.
Describe the air like a magic trick that has no answer.
Describe wonder like dreams you forget as soon as you wake up.
Describe the universe like a bubble blown by a little girl on the street.

◆ SHANNON ROSE, age 13

A UNIVERSE OF IDEAS

Describe an eclipse like segregation
shadowing all freedom.
Describe the moon like a child's eyes
with a shimmer of longing hope.
Describe the galaxy like a set of teeth
waiting to be brushed by the wind.
Describe the Earth like a golf ball
in a field of shooting stars.
Describe the universe like a quilt
with a border of stars and love.

◆ LEAH ESTRELLA, age 10

CONSTELLATION

Describe the Earth like a fish
swimming through an ocean of stars.
Describe the galaxy like a baby
sucking his thumb of gravity
while being rocked to sleep.
Describe the Little Dipper like a kid
wandering through a forest of planets and darkness.
Describe constellations like coats of bright lights
waiting to be worn.

◆ SCOTT CHILBERG, age 13

THE GALAXY

Describe the Earth like a tie-dyed shirt
worn by the solar system.
Describe the galaxy like a waterfall
washing its stars like waves
on the beach of the universe.
Describe the Big Dipper like wisteria
crawling its bright leaves over the stars.
Describe the moon like a snail
stretching its head over the horizon
just as the sun sets.

◆ LYDIA ROWETT, age 11

DESCRIBE THE SEA

Describe the sea like an eagle,
crashing through the ocean of air.

Describe the sand like powdered sugar
being lightly sprinkled on a plate of waffles.

Describe the sun like a banana,
laughing at the grape of the moon.

Describe seaweed like slimy fingers,
brushing back watery hair from your eyes.

◆ SARAH GREINER, age 9

A River Sounds Like a Book

Choose a **subject**. You might write about music, a sport, a food, something that grows outside, a body of water, an object in the sky, an animal, a place, or a feeling.

Then write a poem about your subject, telling some of the following. Tell what it:

feels like	sings like	draws like	tastes like	sounds like
dreams like	moves like	hears like	writes like	sees like
talks like	thinks like	dances like	looks like	paints like

E X A M P L E :   MY RIVER WRITES
A river races like an alphabet ready to spell
and feels like paper, dripping with ideas.
A river sounds like pages turning in a book,
and smells like ink floating on stones.
My river hears like characters in a novel
and looks like the stage of a play.
Some mornings, my river composes like a fountain pen,
writing a raft of ideas.

Write your poem on the following lines:

_____

_____

_____

_____

_____

_____

_____

_____

_____

_____

THE DESERT

The desert is dry like a tasteless burger
and looks like a mound of unanswered questions
jumbled together.

The desert sounds like a bunch of popcorn
in the pot and smells like a cloudy night.

The desert draws like an upside-down rainbow,
giggling in a fit of laughter, telling jokes to his friends—
cloud, hail, snow, and thunder.
It remembers like a harsh wind across a prairie
and sings like a rusty rope, old like the dust of a castle.

The desert dreams about its younger days
when its voice was as pretty as bells
and soft as silk.

◆ DANIEL KERVRAN, age 10

PREJUDICE

Prejudice is cruelty.
It is cold like the north wind
freezing your personality in its tracks.

Prejudice seems like your life
is getting crushed,
like peanut brittle.

Prejudice hurts like iron rods
whipping you into shreds.

Some people become like pyramids
and prejudice is one of the stones.

◆ VICTOR LINDSTROM, age 11

STARS

Stars move like armor,
blasting through a silky wall
of the solar system.
Stars feel like a snake-like rubber,
flaming of planets.
Stars look like golden brown hot dogs,
lying in space.
Stars hear like radios,
announcing about Earth.
Stars love like little hamsters,
munching on the gases of the universe.
They think like mice scrambling for cheese.
Stars sing like birds
in a blizzard of happiness.
Stars hope for more starships to come
to take them to Earth.

◆ JAMES CHRISTIANSON, age 10

I Used to Be Like a Lightbulb

Complete the following sentences adding the names of things, such as seasons, foods, months, animals, transportation, bodies of water, sports, objects in your house, and things in the forest.

EXAMPLES: I used to be like an old car, stuck in reverse and going backwards.
Now I am like a helicopter, traveling easily in all directions.

I used to be like _____

_____

Now I am like _____

_____

I used to be like _____

_____

Now I am like _____

_____

I used to be like _____

_____

Now I am like _____

_____

I used to be like _____

_____

Now I am like _____

_____

I used to be like _____

_____

Now I am like _____

On another sheet of paper, use your favorite lines in a poem.

BACK IN THE DAYS WHEN I WAS YOUNG

When I was young,
I used to be a baby koala,
not knowing what I was doing,
but now I am like an owl,
keeping an eye on whatever comes my way.

When I was young, I wasn't very fast.
I was like a pond always slowing.
Now I'm like a river forever flowing.

When I was young, I wasn't very stable.
I'd fall and stumble,
but now I'm older and wiser.
I'm like a jungle with a thousand lions.
Hear my roars rumble.
In fact, I used to be like a dolphin.
I'd roam the ocean.

Now I'm like magic, a secret potion.

◆ ARTHUR B. SORIANO, age 13

ONCE I WAS LIKE THE MOON

I wasn't always like the spring,
surrounded by rebirth.
Once I was like the winter,
my heart frozen solid.

I wasn't always like a galaxy,
my stars capturing the wonder of gazers.
Once I was like an ominous black hole
drawing the light into my darkness.

I wasn't always like the sun,
joining others in the wonders of day.
Once I was like the moon,
staring at everyone as they slept,
the waves creating a brand-new shore,
the beach torn apart by the sea,
a seedling hidden from the sun
by those much stronger.

◆ BROOKE CALLIHAN, age 16

I USED TO BE

I used to be like a brook, so narrow and defined.
Now I am like a delta, open to all possibilities.
I used to be like a locked door, shutting everyone out.
Now I am like a beckoning hand, wanting you to play.
I used to be like a fire, wild and destructive.
Now I am like a stove, full of heat well contained.
I used to be like an unplanted seed with no chances.
Now I am like a flower, ready to bloom.

◆ AARON LOUX, age 12

Sometimes Fear Is Like an Arrow

Choose a **subject** for your poem. Some possibilities are sports, music, hobbies, things found in nature, feelings, and manufactured objects. Write your subject on the lines below after the words *sometimes* and *other times*.

In the following example, the subject of the poem is *story*. The story is compared to a train and a volcano. The characteristics of the train and volcano are used to describe a story. Use the traits of the second nouns in your comparisons to describe the subject of your poem. Write your descriptions on the blank lines below.

E X A M P L E :   STORY
Sometimes a story is like a train.
Stop. Start. Forward. Back.
Can't find the ticket.
Windows won't open.
Oh no, I've missed my stop.
Other times a story is like a volcano.
Words crumble and reshape,
pick up ash, lava-hot ideas
sizzling the banks of memory.

Sometimes _____ is like _____

_____

_____

_____

_____

Other times _____ is like _____

_____

_____

_____

 On another sheet of paper, use your subject and your descriptions in a poem. You may want to include other ideas.

MY DAY

Sometimes my day is like an illusion.
Abracadabra,
a crystal ball shatters
and becomes birds.
The stage lights up
and time begins to disappear.

Other times my day is like a dream.
Wonders come to life
and nightmares vanish.
Images of people
become a five-second story.

◆ VINCENT HO, age 12

ON SATURDAY

Sometimes Saturday is like a hammock,
slow and lazy, swinging back and forth,
steady and warm in the golden light.
Hours easily slipping away
cradling you in your sleep, you daydream
in no hurry, folding into the wind.

Other times Saturday is like a waterfall,
going faster and faster,
falling until you hit the water
and you are sucked beneath the surface
in a swirling tunnel of emotions.

◆ RACHEL LEADON, age 13

SCHOOL

Sometimes school is like a noodle,
long and difficult to slurp.
Other times school is like tennis.
The teacher bounces back and forth,
math, science, history,
and I just blink.

◆ TANI IKEDA, age 13

DREAMING

Sometimes a dream is like a roller coaster.
It speeds up and slows down,
scares you, yet is fun.
A dream twists and turns
spins you around and makes you dizzy.
Then it suddenly stops.

Other times a dream is like an ocean.
It's long and almost endless,
shallow at first,
then deeper and deeper.
It carries you off into a calm drifting
and slowly comes back to land.

◆ ALISA WALKER, age 14

SO NERVOUS

Sometimes a clock is like a bomb
ticking, waiting,
ringing, exploding.
I'm nervous.

Other times, a clock is like a mouse
looking, squeaking,
peeking fast and swiftly,
dodging hands.

◆ HUNTER OLSON, age 11

Verb Imagery

creating mental pictures with verbs

Action verbs create mental pictures in poems. Read the verbs *dance, explode,* and *whisper,* for example, and they evoke immediate and vivid images.

Because action verbs provide description, they can take the place of adjectives in poetry. This is an important substitution. Adjectives usually tell about something, while action verbs show pictures of it, as in the following examples:

She is happy.	*She laughs.*
The lake is pretty.	*The lake shimmers.*

Action verbs also facilitate comparisons in lines of poetry. The following examples use the verbs *sprout* or *shift*. Because only certain things sprout or shift, these verbs help determine the kinds of comparisons that can be made:

> *That idea sprouted roots and started to grow.*
> *The sky shifts like a kaleidoscope in a storm.*

Verbs drive the poetry engine. Writers can place this fuel right up front and start lines of their poems with action verbs. Readers, then, are immediately directed to take action, as shown in the following examples:

> *Handle your words with care, or they might break*
> *into unintended meanings.*
> *Race the rain all the way home.*

Action verbs are the athletes of poetry. They run, jump, hurdle, pause, and leap through poems, moving and pacing words and ideas.

Recipe for Basketball

Write a recipe for anything except food. The following are some possible topics:

laughter	softball	playing music	peace
jealousy	soccer	dancing	homework
courage	writing	using the computer	war
creativity	reading	painting	friendship

Then use these and other cooking words to write a **recipe** about your subject.

Begin some or all of your sentences with the highlighted action words, or emphasize them in your poem:

taste	**broil**	**measure**	teaspoon	appetizer
season	**cook**	**add**	cup	dessert
stew	**bake**	**mix**	quart	oven
boil	**spice with**	**sip**	gallon	temperature

FRIENDSHIP

Measure out two people
who know little about each other.
Mix together 1/4 cup of love,
one cup of truth, 1/2 cup of loyalty,
and two cups of kindness.
Stir till smooth and thick.
Bake until it is a cake of friendship.

To make frosting,
mix together some laughter,
a little sadness, some joy,
a cup of inspiration,
and a quart of happiness.
Stir until smooth.

Spread onto the cake.
Slice in half and give one piece
to each of the people.
◆ TAYLOR HILLS, age 11

RECIPE FOR LAUGHTER

Stewing inside you,
Feel the steam tickle down your chin.
Smirk at the smell simmering in your nose.
Let a teaspoon trickle on your tongue.
See how it bakes in your stomach.
Raise the temperature of your heart.
Contain till it boils over your body.
Watch how contagious it is
as you serve out the portions.
Let laughter become your main dish.
◆ CAROLINE KELLY, age 14

RECIPES

Stew of jealousy,
a recipe draining off friendship,
heaping with anger
and a sprinkling of worry,
baked in sadness,
cooked into guilt,
dry of all happiness.

Cake of success,
made of inspiration,
cooked into ideas
mixed with perseverance,
all doubt strained out,
heat until ready to consume.
◆ CHRIS NOVICK, age 16

BASEBALL

Here's the recipe for how to play baseball—
Get two teams of nine players.
Heat up the crowd, so they start to boil.
Add three teaspoons of bases
and a cup of home plate.
Measure out a few gallons of grass,
and season with dirt and a little chalk.
Give it an appetizer of two bull pens
and a main course of dugouts.
Throw in a dessert
of a few bats, a ball, and mitts,
and you're ready to play ball.
◆ ALEXANDER DAWSON, age 9

Hear the Rhythm

Choose a type of music, an animal, a sport, a feeling, weather, something that grows, an object in the sky, or some other topic for the subject of your poem.

Write your **subject** on the following line:

Then write a poem about your topic. **Start** some or all of your sentences with the following verbs, or put the word I before them:

| Hear | Feel | Touch | Taste | Sing |
| See | Smell | Move | Know | Listen to |

E X A M P L E :   CATCH
Hear the crack of the ball against wood.
Taste the hope of the batter.
See, in slow motion,
my legs chest-high, acrobatic roll,
glove raised as the ball nestles
hamburger-like in the bun of my mitt.

LISTEN TO HER WORDS

Listen to the words of Mother Nature.
Hear her dismay.
Sing and dance with the unlucky trees,
and make them feel special.
Then paint a portrait
of how the world should be
and let that be your living theater's background.
◆ ASHLEE HOLTMAN, age 13

SOCCER

Smell the scent of the freshly lined field.
Feel the rush as the referee
blows the whistle to start.
Move to the ball
as it's kicked in your direction.
Listen to the crowd
when your team scores a goal.
Taste the thought of victory.
You hold the lead
with only two minutes left.
◆ CHRIS TOWE, age 13

WORLD SERIES

Feel the pressure.
See the pitcher.
Stare him down in the bottom of the ninth.
Grip the bat with both hands.
Move into the batter's box.
Hear the ball whistling towards you.
Listen to your bat crack hard against it.
Know it's going to be a home run.
Realize what you have done.
Dance around the bases.
◆ KEVIN GARBER, age 13

HUNGRY

I walk on the ocean, and it nibbles at my feet.
I feel the lake. Fish run through my fingers.
I gargle the river, healing all my pains.
I watch night, dawning above my head.
I drink the desert, draining all the sand.
I eat the sky, yes every bit of it.
◆ KAROL NEAVOR, age 9

ELEPHANT'S DANCE

I hear the dance of the elephant—
See his movement
Listen to the rumble of thunder
crashing between his toes

Smell the fire burning within.
◆ BEKA SIMMONS, age 12

Take Off the Rain

Start your poem with one of the following words or use a related word:

Wear   Put on   Take off   Remove

Then add the name of something you do not actually wear. The following are some possibilities:

sky	wind	a book	peace	laughter
the universe	an avalanche	music	hope	rage
stars	a river	a poem	patience	courage

Write a poem about your subject, using the characteristics of the words you've named in it.

EXAMPLE: CLOTHED IN POEMS
Wear poems like gloves.
Reach forward and let them hold
your windy ideas, knit like night
and woven of honesty.

Put on poetry.
It's a shirt for your heart,
glasses for sight,
and a hat to hold your ideas.
Hair dancing, poetry combs your mind.

FLOWER IN THE NIGHT

Wear the heat.
      Flames fall, stars ignite.
         Dance, jump, burn
Is there a difference, hot or cold?
The fire of passion
melts the sky
    TO BE ALIVE

Be a rumpus
      Boom! Shake!
That's the individual!
Vibrant, colorful, and flamboyant.
Do not be a mouse
squeaking in vain
Yell from the stomach!
Demand to be heard!
Look, hear, understand all
    TO BE ALIVE

Describe like an elephant
Stand large and tall
proud to be you.
Be noticed now!
    TO BE ALIVE
    ◆ STEPHANIE PAYNE, age 16

CLOTHES OF THE EARTH

Put on the night sky like a giant cloak
and try on dawn as a veil.
Wear the rainbow like a headband
and water for sandals.
Pierce the sun and the moon on your ears
or use pieces of them on your nails as polish.
Sew the grass as a dress,
and wear the clouds as a belt.
String the trees for a crown
and flowers for jewelry.
Then don the seasons as perfume.
    ◆ JAMIE WHELLER, age 11

WEAR NATURE

You remove the sky
like the warmth of your blanket.
Put on the stars as a pair of pants.
Wear the wind close to your heart like a sweater.
Put on rain like brushing your teeth.
Nature gives you strength
to live another day.
    ◆ TRAVIS WELLS, age 11

WORLD OF POSSIBILITY

Remove the weight of the universe
from your shoulders.
Take off the rage you feel against the world.
Wear hope and put on laughter.

There is a world of possibility,
but it is useless if you're not part of it.
    ◆ CHRIS TOWE, age 13

MUSIC

Wear music like a raincoat
repelling the world's everyday sadness.
Use it to forget your worries,
and go off to faraway places.
Put on a saxophone like a cloak of laughter.
Take off rage and wear a clarinet of joy.
Let dancing heal you.
Wear a piano like a hat,
keeping you warm
even on the wind's worst day.
    ◆ CARMEN M. VIGIL, age 11

Pianos Stitch Sound

Choose a subject for your poem. **Nature, planets, sports,** and **feelings** are topics that work particularly well with these words.

Begin some or all of your sentences with the highlighted action words or emphasize them in your poem:

weave	**knit**	design	fabric
sew	**repair**	pattern	sewing machine
stitch	**quilt**	thread	yarn
needlepoint	needle	blanket	textures

E X A M P L E :   FABRIC OF AUTUMN
Trees weave leaves into the fabric of autumn
on the loom of October.
Their threads pattern strips of bark
and quilt with the leather of roots.
Each time it rains,
new patterns form,
firm and breathing,
like music, like hope.

MOTHER NATURE

Mother Nature sighs
as she starts to repair the Year.
The Year has forgotten her coat again
and she is cold and bare.

Mother Nature knits a design
of pink buds and green swirls of mist.
When Mother Nature finishes the last tree,
she weaves in all the wonders of the world.

Little yellow birds flitter under her needle
as Mother Nature adds texture,
then humans,
then love.

◆ SYLVIE KREKOW, age 10

THE FABRIC OF BASEBALL

The bat stitched its way to the ball
like a needle, diving into a quilt.
As it connected, it soared
through the sunset woven sky,
and out of the park it went.
The whole blanket of fans
got louder and louder
as they watched the ball
rise over their heads,
higher and higher.

◆ SEAN KEELEY, age 13

WINTER'S DESIGN

Strands of a summer breeze woven tightly together
with a lining of the iciest air
make the hem of a cold winter wind.

Snow is sewn of soft comforter feathers,
matched carefully with freezing fluff.

Winter's design is patterned with bare trees,
reaching their loom-like branches
trying unsuccessfully to catch
the slippery threads of hail
and weave it into a pillowcase of ice.

◆ HANNAH PAGE-SALISBURY, age 10

NEEDLEPOINT LIKE THE STARS

Needlepoint like the stars
patterns of animals and gods
watching over us
when the lights are low.
Hold us, a solitary people,
in the beauty of the night.

◆ EMILY WALSH, age 14

Alliteration, Consonance, and Assonance

Repetition of sounds that organize poetry and give it unity

A L L I T E R A T I O N is the repetition of initial consonant sounds, as in the following examples:

> *Serious snakes slink* through the fields.
> *Take* that *tattered* letter *to* the office *today.*

A small amount of alliteration in a poem often spreads the connotations of the sounds subtly through the writing. A lot of alliteration frequently provides humor and emphasizes sound. Ask students to generate lists of words, each word on a list starting with the same initial consonant sound. This gives students great opportunities to use the dictionary to expand their writing vocabularies. Then have students name the connotations of some of the initial sounds. *S* words (called **sibilance**), for example, often seem sliding, silky, and soft.

C O N S O N A N C E is the repetition of consonant sounds occurring anywhere in words, and alliteration is a form of consonance. The term consonance, however, usually refers to the repetition of consonant sounds in the middle or at the ends of words, as in the sentence "He *rolled* the *ball slowly* down the lane." Consonance establishes a satisfying repetition that spreads the connotation of sounds through poems. It reinforces the meanings of words without forcing the focus on sound.

A S S O N A N C E is the repetition of vowel sounds in words with different controlling consonants, as in *rope* and *home.* Assonance creates **near** or **off rhyme**, which is quite similar to **exact rhyme.** Assonance, like end rhyme, stresses vowels and unifies poetry through sound, as in the sentence "She *sleeps* and *dreams* of *greetings* from her friends."

Sounds make poems seem silly or serious. They throw open the poetry doors. Then they subtly or boldly enter, announcing that sound is a form of meaning.

She Seemed Certain Her Shadow Was Following Her

Choose a **subject** beginning with the sound of *sssss*. The following are some possibilities:

sail	sailboat	salmon	sun	the sea
skiing	science	sand	soccer	space
setback	shadow	shortcut	snow	story

Then write a poem about it that makes sense, using some of the words in the lists on this page and including other words that begin with the sound of *sssss*.

shady	silly	certain	serious	soft
silky	silver	sliver	secure	season
silent	snake-like	satin	save	sound
sliding	sophisticated	separate	simple	still

E x a m p l e :   SCIENCE FICTION
I love science fiction,
With snake-like precision,
it winds me round in its story.
I sit still in front of my screen
determined this time not to scream
as it slides through my fears
like lightning slipping off a cliff.

Science fiction is the season of suspense,
an autumn of anticipation.
It grows like the finest silk,
a seamless, snug fit for my senses.

SEASON

A shortcut across the soft silent field
brings us to the end of the space
where soaked blades sink wet into my shoes.
It shows us the awesome scape,
serious shadows that want
to tell a story of sight and sound.

We stare, scared, not of it
but of how to save this sad,
satin green of still leaves.

We stare so long,
we soar our sights,
over wants and needs and self
to a separate yet similar season of serenity.

◆ VERA GIAMPIETRO, age 14

SPRING

The sparrow soars in the bright new sky
while the spring lies silvery below.
Chutes of grass start to see the sun
and the last of the new spring snow.

The sun sets low in the darkening sky
and the stars begin to appear.
The satiny darkness spreads softly
as slivers of light sneak through our fears.

◆ STACEY CAREW, age 16

MOUNTAINS

Sweat-stained climbers
vicious peaks
ascending slowly
tedious weeks

Isolated struggle
serious fights
to savor soaring
snow-soaked heights

Separately snaking
up routed to the tops
of sugar-soft mountains,
no sitting, no stops.

◆ ERIC FICKENSCHER, age 16

Sipping on lips slowly
the taste is like syrup
sliding down your heart.

Sighs of contentment, silly smiles,
sly shy sideways glances—
it's all a part of a serene kiss.

◆ TANI IKEDA, age 13

Predictable Pretzels

Choose a subject for your poem that begins with the letter *p*. **Then write a poem about the subject that makes sense,** including many words that start with *p*.

The following are some words you might include in your poem:

patient	prove	progress	point	particular
polite	predictable	passionate	patient	pretty
prized	promise	programmed	plain	produce
precise	puzzled	possibility	pens	pencil
prejudice	poems	pretentious	pretense	power

EXAMPLE: POEMS

Pens dare us to write poems
about porcupines, possums, and plums,
find prizes in vowels,
walk along the perimeters of stars,
and parade world after world
in a panoply of word paint.

PROMISES

People make promises full of power
and children think of them as prized possessions.
Promises, though, can be pretentious,
putting forth false guarantees.
Some children wait patiently
for a particular promise to be fulfilled.

These children believe,
and so they wait,
passionate to prove to the world
that a promise is worth power
beyond any price.

◆ ASHLEE HOLTMAN, age 13

POSSIBILITY

Possibility is the promise of life,
predictability is not.

The price is not in the programmed
but in passionate people,
without rigidity or prejudice.

◆ RICK ABENDROTH, age 16

PONDERING PARALLELS

Petite, pretty princesses
parade pensively about the palace,
passionately praying for plump princes' promises.

Plain peasants patiently peel potatoes
and provide other provincial tasks.

People ponder possible parallels
between these puzzling worlds.

◆ MEGHAN BARNES, age 16

TELL

Tell the world about putrid prejudice,
people's prospects,
souls dying in their eyes.
The price of distinct looks—
people piercing your potential,
pointing out color.

◆ BIANCA TOLUA, age 13

PUZZLES

Patient minds probe puzzles.
People pass their pencils over crosswords,
use brain power to prove precise on jigsaws,
penetrate riddles.
People particularly like to be puzzled.

◆ MEGAN FLAHERTY, age 13

Open Road

All of the words in the following lists contain the sound *oh.*

Choose one of these words or another word with the sound *oh* for the subject of your poem.

On the lines at the bottom of the page, **write a poem that makes sense,** including words with the sound of *oh*.

stone	roam	flown	remote	motion
jolt	thrown	demote	promotion	noticeable
own	only	opened	tone	toast
boast	ocean	rode	road	unknown
notify	show	float	occasion	Ohio

EXAMPLE: PROMOTION?
We would like to notify you
that you have received a promotion.
However, the job will keep you on the open road
ten months out of the year.
You will be flown to places you do not know,
exposed to hundreds of opinions,
shown incomplete records.
Your clients will seem remote
and noticeably moan at meetings.
Congratulations on your promotion!

OCTOBER

October is a beautiful word,
like the crack of oak
and frozen gold.

With words like *spring* and *maybe*
only the lips and tongue are wanted,
wanted but not needed.

October requires a commitment
that rolls from the back of the throat
echoes in the chest and
makes the muscle of a
strong heart ache sweetly.

October holds the smoky distances
of long nights,
the honest work of
a hard love

that stays soft and fluid
when the snows come and
the rivers draw low.

◆ CLAUDIA MAURO, adult

THROWN FROM A BOAT

Last time I rode in a boat,
it was on the open ocean.
I dipped in my toe and was thrown
by the jolt of a noticeable motion.
I hit a stone and floated alone.

I thought I was toast
but my mom used her cell phone
to notify the medics.
I was flown by helicopter to Ohio.

When I awoke, I didn't know my name
My head had been hit by the stone
and the bump had grown,

and my rescuer boasted of his promotion.

◆ TYLER PECKENPAUGH, age 11

THE STONE

A stone boasted about his place under a tree.
He said, "No one can move me."
Then he was tossed, thrown into the sea.
Now mostly he groans and moans
though occasionally he boasts
about his place,
under the sea.

◆ KATHLEEN COMPTON, age 12

THIS ROAD

This road was very long
and sometimes I wished I would have flown.
Most of the time I was alone.
After a while, I couldn't feel my toes
and I asked myself,
Where does it end?
But I thought,
Nobody knows.
So I kept walking and walking.
I looked at myself and realized I had grown
but I kept walking,
walking into the unknown.

◆ KYLE BANTA, age 13

Sound Packed

All of the words in the following lists contain the sound at the beginning of the word *at*.

Write a poem that makes sense, using these and other words that contain this sound:

crack	battle	patch	capture	practical
catcher	fact	factual	absence	action
applesauce	racket	package	manage	rap
average	absolute	magic	match	ladder
attack	map	strategy	practice	laughter
fattening	apple	match	rattlesnake	rattle

E X A M P L E :   SMILE ATTACK
The smile strategy worked like magic.
They managed to get the same amount done,
gave up climbing the ladder of fear,
and replaced it with an open circle.
Complaints were no match for the smiles.
Longtime cracks in friendship
magically sealed with this glue of laughter.

HAPPY ATTACK

Laughter is like a happy attack,
a very practical action.
If at battle with yourself
practice your laugh,
capture the absolute magic of laughter.
It's a fact if you are sad,
you can catch the feeling of happiness,
answer a joke,
giggle with friends.
There's no match to a good laugh.

◆ MEGAN FLAHERTY, age 13

EATING APPLESAUCE

While eating applesauce,
he made quite a racket.
He made the sounds of laughter
and slurping like a practical rap.

No one had the heart to tell him
that his manners lacked tact.
For it was a fact,
that the average, normal laugh
did not shake a household.

◆ TATIANA WESTIN-McCAW, age 13

LAUGH

I hear laughter,
and it captures my attention.
Some people might call it a racket,
just a lot of noise.
But later when I am alone,
the absence of laughter
is deafening to my ears.

When I laugh, my voice cracks.
It's a fact that some people
think I am strange.
Part of me wants them to accept me,
but another part says,
Who cares?
It is a battle of opinions,
and the war rages inside me.

◆ ARIANA PETERSON, age 12

MAGIC TEACHER

I am the teacher of magic.
Now remember, if you are a maniac,
you may not take this class.
First, I conjured this map this morning.
If you manage to draw a match for this map
by using only maple syrup,
you shall receive points
that you can cash in for a shelling machine
or perhaps a Mack truck.
Oh my, the time has flown.
Class dismissed. Good Day.

◆ JOSH RICHARDS, age 14

Campfire

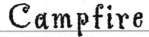

Choose a **subject** that contains the letter *m*. The following are some possibilities:

time	romance	salmon	somersault	comment
comment	rhythm	game	dome	emotion
fame	memory	smoke	cinema	gem

Then write a poem about the subject that makes sense, using some of the words in the lists on this page or including other words that contain the letter *m*.

team	seem	simmer	remember	somewhere
palm	calm	game	glimmer	promote
tumble	moment	smash	tomorrow	timing
smoky	slumber	mammoth	camp	poem

EXAMPLE: CINEMA
Cinema is an emotional gem,
remote enough for comfort,
yet so close I can hold images in my hands.
Through movies, I feel hope tumbling fresh as popcorn,
taste fear like the texture of smoke,
and hear courage as bold as a poem written by a storm.
Then it ends and as if by magic,
I resume my composure.
But all through the day,
I open my hands and let the cinema
play again in my palms.

SMOKY AIR

Someone asked you to comment
on the problem with smokers.
You said, "Smart people don't smoke."
What did you mean?

Monstrous waves of carbon monoxide,
stinky smells from the end of that snake.
That's what I think.

Seems to me, the world has a problem,
and the first thing to do is crumble it.

◆ MAEGAN KUMP, age 13

SOMETIMES

Sometimes, rain becomes a door
and no longer afraid of getting wet,
we step in and become fluid in the moment.
Sometimes, fear becomes an opening
and we imagine meeting the fire
of our worries with truth
and somehow we do not get burned.
Sometimes, laughter becomes a window.
The shutters are no longer comfortable,
and it just becomes too much work
remembering how to see in the dark.

◆ SOPHIE SINGER, adult

SALMON

Imagine a salmon in a river,
splashing out of the water
forming a calm, shimmering rainbow.

Remember a mountain like a camp tent.
Nearby, a salmon swims so fast,
jumping like a flame.

◆ KIRSTEN FUKUHARA, age 10

FLAME IGNITES

The fire roars in the room
as it sends a glimmer of light
throughout the house.

The moment the flame ignites,
the dog starts barking,
like the clamor of dishes
breaking on the ground.

◆ CLIVE MUNZ, age 10

BMX

BMXing is a smash
roaming the skate park
trying to get mammoth air,
your sweaty palms on the grips.
You had to get the timing right
on your tricks but instead you tumbled
on the smoky colored cement floor,
somewhat mangled on the ground.
Memories of that time are emotional.

◆ CHAD MOORE, age 14

Synesthesia

The description of one sensory perception by another

S Y N E S T H E S I A evokes one sense with another. *Taste the sky, hear the cloud,* and *see that sound* are examples of synesthesia. With synesthesia, colors are heard, sounds touched, and smells seen. Synesthesia is highly figurative language that does not lend itself to academic explanation. Rather, synesthesia works best when sensed.

Try this exercise with your students to give them an experience of synesthesia. Write the following lists on the board or display them on an overhead projector:

touch	see	hear	taste	smell
the sky	a sound	stars	January	music
the night	a taste	perfume	joy	the alphabet
hope	March	Mars	an asteroid	a rainbow
summer	a smell	red	the day	words

Tell your students that there is a sense word at the top of each list that does not literally describe the nouns listed below it. Ask a student to read a sensory word, name a word in the column below it, and extend the sentence, as in *Hear red talking about fire.*

Repeat the process with other students. For an extra challenge, students might add their own words to the columns, generating additional examples of synesthesia.

Poets enjoy writing synesthesia. Using a recipe that mixes the senses, synesthesia has the recognizable taste of poetry.

I Am So Hungry for Red

On the lines below, **start** your poem with the following words, or use a variation:

> I am so hungry for

Then name a color. Tell why you are hungry for that color.

Name things that are the color or give its traits.

You might include some of these verbs: *chew, sip, digest, drink, taste, slurp, eat.*

E X A M P L E :   BLUE
I am so hungry for blue,
quick and clear
like a stream of possibilities.
I want to chew blue slowly
and feel the river and sky in me.
Sometimes, I become raven,
that acrobat and joker.
Other times I am salmon
climbing blue like a rope,
skipping up, Double Dutch
towards the sky.

_____

_____

_____

_____

_____

_____

_____

_____

_____

_____

_____

ORANGE

I am so hungry for the color orange
like an octopus that has been stuck in the sea.
It has arms of summer
and feet of fall.

Orange dreams about the kids
who play in the spring air
and talks about dripping
into a river of August.

Orange inhales the fall breeze
that flows in my window.

◆ PARKER COLEBROOK, age 11

HUNGRY FOR YELLOW

I am so hungry for yellow
bright and smiling
like the arc of a banana.

I want to bask in its warmth,
study it in the night sky
with a powerful microscope
and give the yellow of the rose
grown from the heat of the sun.

◆ MARY PATTERSON, age 16

GREEN

I am so hungry for green
Swaying softly in the wind
Like a tree standing alone.
I want to roll down green hills
Totally free from the restraints of society
Or swim in the sea-green pools,
Allowing the cool water
To wash away my anxieties.
I long for the freedom of green
And mourn its disappearance.

◆ MARK NIEMANN, age 16

GRAY

I'm hungry for gray
dull and long like an October day.
I want to grab gray,
yet I am afraid of what dreams may come
from the simple touch of it.
I'm hungry for gray,
yet no matter how dark and mysterious,
gray will always be an outcast among colors.

◆ CHRIS GARCIA, age 14

RED HUNGER

I am so hungry for red,
burning down my throat.
I want to feel red's power
well up inside me,
dance upon a candle's flame,
feel the heat in my hands,
as if I were holding the sun
in my grasp.

◆ AARON LOUX, age 12

Sip Autumn

Choose a **subject** for your poem that has nothing to doing with eating or food. The following are some possibilities:

friendship	wonder	night	a rainbow	soccer
love	family	summer	stars	music
envy	life	dawn	the sky	the piano
the past	time	midnight	the sun	a computer

Write your subject on the following line:

_____

Start your poem with one of these verbs that relate to food and beverages:

Taste   Chew   Digest   Sip   Drink   Gobble   Slurp   Savor   Eat

Then write a poem about your subject, using the verbs listed above to describe it.

EXAMPLE:

TASTE THE SKY
Digest the sky.
Use the moon as a bowl,
and sun for your cup.
Eat a rainbow.
It tastes like ice cream.
Munch stars like peanut brittle
and savor the mashed potato clouds.
Gulp the sky. It flavors your days and nights.

_____

_____

_____

_____

_____

_____

_____

_____

THE TASTE OF INFORMATION

Sip the monitor
and use the mouse as your cup.
Bring the keyboard close and gobble it
like Thanksgiving dinner.
Slurp the cords and cables
with a flavor of licorice in your mouth.
Taste the information.
It will give you an electromagnetic, energetic day.
 ◆ JENNIFER THAVISETH, age 13

DIGEST LIFE

Munch the stars,
Bright like your thoughts.
Digest music communicating with you.
Drink the rain soothing your emotions.
Taste the sky full of possibilities.
Gobble life, and live it to the fullest.
 ◆ CHRIS TOWE, age 13

BAD TASTE

Chew envy and grind it in the midnight stream.
Swallow the parts of lies that scratch the purity of life.
Choke on the rumors that clutter
the beauty of bonds and friendships.
Lick the nonsense off the rocks of jealousy.
Sip the taste of hatred
molding to the hearts of everyone it enters.
 ◆ SERINA BOISJOLIE, age 14

TASTE TIME

Chew the past
Munch it like Cheerios
Savor happy days like sugar
And slurp sad ones like eggnog
Digest the future when put on your plate
Think of laughter as chocolate
And tears like seeds
Nourish them into memories.
 ◆ MIKE PHILLIPS, age 14

Before You Can Touch the Night

Start your poem with the words:

Before you (can)

Add an action word. The following are some possibilities:

see	know	hear	dream	touch	feel
taste	paint	dance	sing	tell	listen to

Then add the name of something you cannot literally see, taste, feel, etc., such as some of the following:

the sky	the night	the day	a rainbow	day
a cloud	fire	earth	wind	a dream
a memory	inspiration	creativity	courage	peace

Develop your idea in a poem.

E X A M P L E : Before you can touch the night,
lift the curtains of curiosity.
Feel midnight's texture tight as a star
and light as the cellophane moon.
Before you can paint the day,
prepare the palette of your ideas.
Then grab a sun ray as a paintbrush
and splash colors scattered in play.

_____

_____

_____

_____

_____

_____

_____

_____

PORTRAIT

Before you paint my portrait,
touch my heart,
feel my breath,
taste my emotions,
play my thoughts,
dance my envy,
dream my ambition,
Masterpiece.

◆ BIANCA TOLUA, age 13

Before you can touch the day,
listen to those who call you.
Sing and hear your voice,
painted on the airwaves of life.

Before you can dream,
remember the times of the day.
Then hear who talks to you
at night when you're asleep.

◆ MATTHEW BACH, age 13

YOUR STORY

Before you can dance,
you need a sea of fire.

Before you can see,
you need stars for eyes.

Before you can swim,
you need the fishes' fins.

Before you can draw the world,
you need a rainbow of colors.

Before you can tell,
you need the wind to guide your story.

◆ MELISSA CHEN, age 8

THE NIGHT

Before you can feel the night
you must wash your hands with the stars.
Dry them with the midnight rush.
Feel the sleepy texture of its cold breath.
Then let go with the break of day.

◆ ANDREA CASASBEAUX, age 10

BEFORE YOU BLAME

Before you condemn someone
step inside her shoes.

Before you know you're right
look at it from another perspective.

Before you blame
remember the fire of criticism scorches.

Before you ridicule
listen closely to the story.
It might sound just like yours.

◆ SALLY SODERBERG, adult

Mood with Prepositions

Prepositions are words that show relationship between a subject and object

Poets generally establish M O O D (feeling, attitude, or ambiance) in writing through their choices of nouns, verbs, and adjectives. Prepositions, on the other hand, are rarely noticed in poems, yet they are poetic gems. A P R E P O S I T I O N is a word that shows the relationship of a subject to a time, place, direction, or amount. Prepositions are listed below under each of these categories:

time	place	direction		amount
after	*against*	*above*	*near*	*with*
before	*in*	*across*	*over*	*without*
during	*inside*	*behind*	*through*	
	out	*below*	*to*	
	outside	*down*	*under*	
		from	*up*	

Ask your students to start their poems with the prepositions *after, before,* or *during*. These words will focus their writing on a time. When students begin lines with the word *in,* attention is riveted on the setting. Starting poems with the prepositions *with* or *without,* or repeating these words in poetry, creates the mood of abundance or scarcity.

In poetry, every word is important. Although prepositions are rarely noticed, poets can intentionally use and repeat them to establish moods in their poems that are both substantial and concrete.

Beyond the City

A preposition can help set a place or mood in poetry. Choose a subject for your poem that names a place or is associated with a particular mood, such as a **sport, season, month, holiday,** or **feeling.**

Then **start** some or all of the sentences in your poem with prepositions in the following lists:

about	around	between	inside *or* in	through
above	before	beyond	of	toward
across	behind	by	off	under
after	below	down	on	up
against	beneath	during	outside	with
among	beside	from	over	without

EXAMPLE: VACATION

Under the sun, you collect moments like seashells.

Beyond language, you understand the conversations of waves.

Above hurry, inside rest, past worry, outside time

you slide into your summer vacation.

_____

_____

_____

_____

_____

_____

_____

_____

_____

_____

_____

AUTUMN

In the autumn,
I go outside and toss the leaves like stars
carelessly scattered through the air.
Between the stars are patches of nighttime.
If you look closely,
you can see a path of peace,
winding its way through war.

On every doorstep,
a pumpkin is embraced in a cloak of orange.
Within myself, a memory of Halloween excitement
creeps through me like a spider.

◆ DANA GOLDEN, age 10

MAGICIAN

On the ears of magic,
deception and illusion
dangle like jewelry.
Hear the music and song
of sleight of hand
and listen to the shiver of smoke
as rabbits and doves appear.

◆ AJA HAMMERLY, age 16

RAINY DAY

Outside, rain beats upon the windows
as September rolls around.
It falls from the leaf
and splashes on the ground.
It slips silently through the house
as the children come in to play
and in mother's shoe it goes
without further delay.

A worm!

◆ SARAH GREINER, age 9

AUTUMN

In the autumn,
leaves fall to the ground
like snowflakes.
They whirl through the crisp air,
their simple beauty
beyond so many other stages in their lives.
Wind and rain clash together
to make a fearsome storm.

◆ HANNAH PAGE-SALISBURY, age 10

FROM THE POINT OF VIEW OF DREAMS

From the point of view of dreams
anything is possible.
To fly like a butterfly is a simple task,
and a nightmare
is just another spin on a ride.
According to dreams, in a short time
a life story can be told.

◆ SYDNEY TOWNES-WETZEL, age 13

Inside Ice

Start with one of the following words:

Inside or **In**

Then add a subject, naming something you would not go inside. The following are some possibilities:

a star	fire	the sun	joy	a piano
a volcano	a tree	a rainbow	courage	a soccer ball
spring	Mars	my body	fear	a computer

Write a poem telling what's inside your subject.

E X A M P L E :   INSIDE THE SUN
Inside the sun a river of light
courses across the sky.
Its rays open like hands gathering
pebble-constellations of stars.
Boats of heat raft the summer nights.
Inside the sun, time seems to melt
but the wick of possibility never cools down.

INSIDE MY BODY

Inside my body,
A galaxy of stars twinkle.
Inside my body,
Rivers of imagination flow.
Inside my body,
A forest of life flourishes.
Inside my body,
It snows intelligence and cleverness.
Inside my body,
There is every color in the world.

◆ AARON LOUX, age 12

BOX OF FEELINGS

In my box of feelings
flowers bloom and die.
Mountains rise with new hopes
and crumble in sadness.
When I'm angry, fires blaze,
when excited, birds sing.
Some hopes are too small to touch the ceiling
while others tower above it.
Nights pass, and days too,
and my box of feelings is never the same.

◆ LAURA SCHREINER, age 12

SEATTLE EARTHQUAKE

Inside my body, I shake
like the earthquake that bounces our room.
It reminds me of a thousand elephants
stampeding towards the school.
The ground of fear explodes like a volcano.
I think I am going to fall apart,
like paper as it moves through a shredder.
Everyone cries and moans,
like the wind on a cold night.

◆ HANNAH KRAJNIK, age 9

INSIDE HOPE

Inside a sunbeam there is lightning
that unleashes fire going to the skies.
Inside a speck is a rainbow
with every color of the world.
Inside love, the flag of our country
tells people every night that peace
is better than fighting and injustice.
Inside the ball of justice,
people pray at midnight.

◆ TAYLOR HALPERIN, age 10

INSIDE SPACE

Inside a sunbeam the sound of love
echoes hope off the walls of light.
Inside a snowflake is a fire of courage
sledding down a hill of happiness.
Inside a rainbow is the memory of peace
shining dreams all over the world.
Inside a star is the voice of a family
strong and solid as a rock.

◆ DANA GOLDEN, age 10

Without Music

Start your poem with the word:

Without

Then add another word. The following are some possibilities:

rain	hope	memory	music	sports
sun	love	the future	sound	fear
night	tears	the past	song	computers
sky	worry	this moment	time	pens

Complete your sentence, and **then write a poem about that idea**. You might also start new sentences using the word *without,* and add thoughts related to your first idea.

E X A M P L E :   WITHOUT THE SUN AND MOON

Without the sun

there would be no shadows.

Where would we hold our fears?

Without the moon,

how would we learn about phases,

the turn of a pen like an idea

changing from crescent to full?

_____

_____

_____

_____

_____

_____

_____

_____

_____

_____

_____

WITHOUT THE SKY

Without the sky,
who would hold the stars
that make our wishes come true?

Who would support the sun
that shines in the darkest corners
revealing truths?

Without its arms,
the body of the sky
would no longer
find within itself
the desire to live,
no longer want
to discover another way
to hold the moon,
the night
or this day.

◆ TRACY RODGERS, age 12

WITHOUT LOVE

Without love,
the dark licks his lips
about to swallow the universe whole.
He starts with all the vile things in the world,
making him stronger.
War willingly goes into the dark,
gobbled up like a meal.
Then dark starts on his dessert.
First he chomps on peace.
When he finishes, he tries to gnaw hope.
But hope joins forces with determination,
and they break through dark,
shattering him and restoring love.

◆ SYLVIE KREKOW, age 10

WITHOUT WAVES

Without waves
you couldn't hear the sunset,
the shore would cease to change,
and boats wouldn't rock passengers to sleep.

Without waves
there would be no sounds, no chords,
there would be no color, no light.

Would we be afraid of the dark?

◆ AJA HAMMERLY, age 16

WITHOUT THE SKY

Without the sky
there would be no night.
Without the night,
there would be no moon,
no stars for children to wish upon,
no wishes to be granted
and nothing to turn to in hope.

◆ KATIE BUSHNELL, age 15

Inquiry

Questioning or close examination

An I N Q U I R Y is a type of questioning, a close examination in search of information or truth. The root of the word *question* is *quest*. An inquiry or question used in poetry leads the writer on a journey or quest of discovery.

Poetry writing is the perfect language to use to ask questions and closely examine ideas. In poetry, student inquiries are as broad as their imaginations. Encourage your students to brainstorm questions for poetry topics. They might inquire, for example:

> *What is the sound of red?*
> *Can people dance in their sleep?*
> *How did the sun get in the sky?*

Like buddies on a field trip, questions and answers are close friends. The questions point out the sights, and the answers quickly respond.

A writer wonders, *What is a smile?* In prose, students often give obvious answers to questions. A student might write that *a smile is a sign of true happiness* or *a smile shows friendship*. In poetry, on the other hand, answers to inquiries seem unlimited. A poet uses figurative and sound language, and the box of likely responses disappears. In poetry, a student might write that *a smile is like the movement of a conductor's baton* or *a smile is the arc of the moon across the face of the sky*.

Why are questions useful in poetry? They act like trampolines, catapulting poets through the roof of predictable answers.

Do You Really Want to Know Me?

Answer the question *Do you really want to know me?*

Start your poem with the words,

If you really want to know me

Then complete the sentence, naming an interest, belief, or feeling.

EXAMPLE OF OPENING SENTENCES:

If you really want to know me, watch me play my saxophone.
My music is like the ocean with changing undercurrents of sound.

Develop your idea by writing more about it. You might repeat the opening line,
If you really want to know me, adding new information.

If you really want to know me _____

_____

_____

_____

_____

_____

_____

_____

_____

_____

_____

_____

_____

_____

_____

KNOW ME

If you really want to know me, look at a rock.

Examine its curves and niches,

sharp edges and smooth planes.

Hold it in your hand and feel its weight,

its solidity and structure.

Toss it in a pond and feel a spray

of water land on your face.

Observe the ripples spreading.

Then try to find the stone.

If you really want to know me,

look at a book filled with hidden messages,

trapped beneath a time-worn cover.

Open it carefully, making sure not to tear it.

Let the words wash over you and fill you up,

like a long conversation with an old friend.

If you really want to know me,

pick up a pair of old pointe shoes.

Feel their damp coating of sweat and smell their odor.

Look at the pink satin, now strings

after hours of labor

   to the sound of a waltz.

     ◆ EMILY WALSH, age 14

CELLO

If you really want to know me,

listen to the soft bass clef sound of my cello

like the ocean sunset, teeming with life.

If you really want to know me,

watch as the vibrating strings make music

like parrots using their vocal cords.

It you really want to know me,

feel in your heart

the deep, deep music

pulsating throughout your body,

like the low rings of a foghorn

sounding in the night.

If you really want to know me,

understand my love for my cello

so strong nothing can break it.

     ◆ SHEA McMANIGAL, age 13

WATCH ME

If you really want to know me

hear me go through an obstacle course at recess.

My passes are like swift winds of agility.

You won't be able to see me, so wait and listen.

If you really want to know me, watch me write my poems.

My pencil is like a jet flying over an ocean

making the words jump up in curiosity.

If you really want to know me, hear me play the piano

as my fingers tap dance across the keys of the music.

Then see the piano dance to the rhythms of sound.

     ◆ AMINE SAOUADI, age 11

What Lives in Your House?

Write about something, other than your family, that lives in your house. The following are some possibilities:

baseballs	justice	joy	books	machines	excuses
chairs	fear	compassion	stories	dishes	ghosts
games	worry	forgiveness	movies	work	history
computers	possibility	responsibility	humor	magic	ideas

Write your subject on the following line, and use that sentence as the first line in your poem.

_____ live(s) in my house.

EXAMPLE: UNCOVERED

Books live in my house.

Sometimes at night, I hear the characters

climb the ladders of words

and slide down the sides of their pages,

to watch TV.

I wish they would vacuum my rug

or take out the trash.

But after I'm asleep, their work is done

and the characters from my favorite stories

sit with their feet up on chairs,

play dominoes, and eat pizza from last night's dinner.

_____

_____

_____

_____

_____

_____

_____

FORGIVENESS

Forgiveness lives in my house,
but she is shy and hard to find.
When she hides, her windows shut out all light.

This forgiveness must be sought
by searching behind the doors.
She sleeps in the closet only to wake
when the blankets of pride and blame are removed.

◆ KATIE BUSHNELL, age 15

GHOSTS

Ghosts live in my house
straining to break free from
things left unsaid
    left undone.
They hang upon our hearts
    cloud our eyes.
They cling to words
traded in empty resolution
between unknown companions
at perfunctory get-togethers.
Ghosts engulf us
    isolating
those we were made to love.

◆ DAVID CALL, age 15

GHOSTS LIVE IN MY HOUSE

Ghosts live in my house
scaring me as I sleep
getting into my dreams at night
making me sigh and weep.

Ghosts live in my house
moving all around
going up and down the hall
barely making sounds.

Ghosts live in my house,
reminding me of the past
talking of their hopes and dreams—
waking me at last.

◆ LEAH ARNOLD, age 12

SOAKED

A sponge lives in my house,
always soaking up my mistakes.
Just let me do it myself.
Next time I spill,
will you have any room
to hold this one too?
Don't you need to dry,
squeeze out and clear yourself
from all the things I've spilled?

I want you to have room
for your messes, too.

◆ HEATHER AQUINO, age 14

What Is Time?

Answer one of the following questions or a similar one using poetic language.
Write what your subject reminds you of or what it is like. Use words in your poems
that are related to your topic. You may ask questions, make statements, or do a
combination of both.

What is electricity?   What is air?   What is a shadow?
What is gravity?   What is thought?   What is the sky?
What is knowledge?   What is light?   What is fire?

EXAMPLE: WHAT IS FIRE?
Is it a flame reshaping
conformity's ashes?
Is it smoke
tired after a long day at work?
Fire is a rain rekindling the earth
and snow that burns on touch.
It is warmth holding an idea
and the volcano's heart at play.
Fire invites you home,
ignites your hope,
then dances, heat rising.

SHADOW

What is my shadow
made of air and stalking me,
tiptoeing through my footsteps,
lurking behind the curve of my head?
I whip around to lash at it
and all that remains is a fading premonition.
I grasp at its dark velvet fringe
as it slips down the wooden stairs,
craving to know it, to know myself.
It is a fleeting moment of my memories,
trapped behind a two-dimensional facade.
It longs to surge and lead
yet constantly is caught in a tearing black riptide
destined forever to hide my self
in the last place I would look,
behind me.

◆ SUSANNE WOOLSEY, age 16

WHAT IS THE SKY?

Is it an endless void
full of possibility and mystery?

It is stars, shining down
on the boy dreaming of going to the moon.

It is rain, pouring out of clouds
like a refreshing shower after a long day.

It is the sun that lights the path.

It is the moon, illuminating the night
making the voyage less lonely.

◆ NICK HAWLEY, age 15

What is electricity?

Is it that spark
connecting people?

Is it that force,
making the world go round?

Electricity is the power that gives you hope.

It is lightning tamed with time.

◆ ANTHONY CAPUTO, age 14

What is the sky?

Is it a protective shield
keeping good things in
and bad out?

Is it a painting,
something to make
the upward glance enjoyable?

The sky is your hopes and dreams,
your goals and spirit, and the promise
that your life will not go unnoticed.

◆ KATHLEEN COMPTON, age 12

Glossary

Alliteration ◆ the repetition of initial consonant sounds

Assonance ◆ the repetition of vowel sounds with different intervening consonants

Consonance ◆ the repetition of consonant sounds anywhere in words

Edit ◆ prepare for publication by adapting, revising, or correcting

Free verse poetry ◆ poetry without end rhyme, set structures, or meter

Imagery ◆ a mental picture

Inquiry ◆ a question

Line break ◆ the place where a line in a poem breaks or ends

Metaphor ◆ the comparison of two unrelated nouns

Mood ◆ the tone of a poem, reflecting the author's attitudes, feelings, and perspective

Personification ◆ the assignment of human traits to things, colors, and ideas

Poem ◆ a compact piece of writing with intentional line breaks whose language expresses an experience, emotion, or aesthetic arrangement of words, usually containing one or more poetic elements

Poetic elements ◆ the fundamentals and foundation of poetry, e.g., metaphor, simile

Preposition ◆ a word that shows the relationship between a subject and an object

Simile ◆ a comparison between two unrelated nouns using "like" or "as"

Stanza ◆ a group of lines separated by a space; similar to a paragraph

Synesthesia ◆ the description of one sensory perception or impression by another

Verse ◆ a line of poetry, a stanza in a poem, or a whole poem

References

WRITING RESOURCE BOOKS

Goldberg, Natalie. *Writing down the Bones*. Boston: Shambhala, 1986.

Graves, Donald. *Writing: Teachers and Children at Work*. Portsmouth: Heinemann, 1983.

Hugo, Richard. *The Triggering Town, Lectures and Essays on Poetry and Writing*. New York: W. W. Norton, 1979.

Jordan, June. *June Jordan's Poetry for the People.* New York: Routledge, 1995.

Koch, Kenneth. *Wishes, Lies, and Dreams: Teaching Children to Write Poetry.* New York: Random House, 1970.

Lakoff, George and Mark Johnson. *Metaphors We Live By.* Chicago: University of Chicago Press, 1980.

Lamott, Anne. *Bird by Bird, Some Instructions on Writing and Life.* New York: Pantheon Books, 1994.

Wallace, Robert. *Writing Poems.* Boston: Little, Brown and Company, 1990.

BOOKS OF POETRY

Bly, Robert, ed. *News of the Universe.* New York: Sierra Club Books, 1980.

Bryan, Ashley. *Ashley Bryan's ABC of African American Poetry*. New York: Simon and Schuster, 1997.

Fleischman, Paul. *Joyful Noise: Poems for Two Voices.* New York: Harper Trophy, 1988.

Hughes, Langston. *The Dream Keeper and Other Poems.* New York, Alfred A. Knopf, 1994.

Moyers, Bill. *The Language of Life, A Festival of Poets.* San Francisco: Doubleday, 1995.

Nye, Naomi Shihab. *Come with Me, Poems for a Journey.* New York: Greenwillow Books, 2000.

Schwartz, Alvin. *A Twister of Twists, A Tangler of Tongues.* New York: J. B. Lippincott Company, 1972.